Redesigning American Education

Redesigning American Education

James S. Coleman, Barbara Schneider,
Stephen Plank, Kathryn S. Schiller,
Roger Shouse, and Huayin Wang
with
Seh-Ahn Lee

Westview Press
A Member of the Perseus Books Group

This book was supported by a grant from the National Science Foundation (RED-9255880). The opinions expressed herein are those of the authors and not the sponsoring agency.

Copyright © 1997 by Westview Press, A Member of the Perseus Books Group

Published in 1997 in the United States of America by Westview Press, 5500 Central Avenue, Boulder, Colorado 80301-2877, and in the United Kingdom by Westview Press, 12 Hid's Copse Road, Cumnor Hill, Oxford OX2 9JJ

A CIP catalog record for this book is available from the Library of Congress
ISBN 0-8133-2495-5 (hc)   ISBN 0-8133-9102-4 (pbk)

The paper used in this publication meets the requirements of the American National Standard for Permanence of Paper for Printed Library Materials Z39.48-1984.

10   9   8   7   6   5   4   3   2

*To James S. Coleman, who trusted us to complete
and publish his ideas for improving America's schools*

Contents

Tables and Figures

Tables

Figures

Acknowledgments

Many individuals and organizations helped to bring this book to completion. We gratefully acknowledge their interest, support, and encouragement. We would especially like to thank the National Science Foundation (NSF) for their support of our project, "Improving Mathematics and Science Learning: A School and Classroom Approach" (grant # RED-9255880). Larry Suter, the NSF project officer for this award, deserves special thanks for his helpful comments, advice, and suggestions.

Next, we thank the Fulbright Scholar Program Grants for U.S. Faculty and Professionals for providing James S. Coleman with support to write a paper while he was a Fulbright Senior Scholar at the European University Institute in 1993, which proved to contain the guiding theoretical principles which underpin this book. We also wish to thank the John M. Olin Foundation for a grant to The George J. Stigler Center for the Study of the Economy and the State at The University of Chicago for additional funding for Stephen Plank and Kathryn Schiller. We also appreciate and recognize the Spencer Foundation's Postdoctoral Fellowship Program for supporting Roger Shouse in completing this work. We are also grateful to Dean Birkenkamp, Vice President at Westview Press at the time we began this project, who encouraged us to initiate and complete this manuscript.

Many excellent comments were received from the Co-Principal Investigator on this NSF grant, Charles Bidwell, and we gratefully acknowledge his insights and suggestions. Additionally, we would like to thank the Ogburn-Stouffer Center Education Studies Group for their comments, and in particular Seh-Ahn Lee, who has been a key collaborator in our work. We also greatly appreciate the helpful criticisms and suggestions of David Stevenson, Senior Adviser to the Under Secretary of Education, U.S. Department of Education. We also thank The University of Chicago, Departments of Education and Sociology, for co-sponsoring a workshop in which Professor Coleman presented his initial ideas.

We thank Debra Milton and Deborah Kulyukin for their help in the preparation of the manuscript and editorial work. A special thanks to Svetlana Durkovic, who has provided editorial and organizational assistance. It's her dedication that finally brought this manuscript to completion. Finally, we thank Cassandra Britton and Leslie Boulay, who have been a tremendous help in getting the manuscript ready for publication, which could not have been completed without their assistance.

Redesigning American Education

1

Incentives for Reforming Schools

Barbara Schneider

Introduction

Despite more than a decade of intensive efforts at school reform, families, teachers, and policymakers continue to demand more effective strategies to improve the academic productivity of American schools. In this book we examine the current organizational structure of public schools and advance several principles for improving the educational system. These principles are based on the fundamental assumption that the present configuration of the public school system reflects traditional bureaucratic concepts of social organizations prevalent in the early part of this century. Arguably, this form of school organization is outmoded and lacks the capacity to accommodate many of the current efforts designed to raise academic performance.

In contrast to this bureaucratic model of schools, a new paradigm is suggested, one that is more congruent with increasing demands for raising academic standards. This model, identified as output-driven, is constructed on the principle that the educational system needs to be reorganized and its resources directed toward increasing student achievement. It recognizes that most student learning occurs in the classroom and that the key to raising academic productivity is developing strong norms that stress student achievement. It would be nearly impossible to instill such norms without strong social ties among teachers and their students. An output-driven system encourages the creation of strong achievement norms by establishing external standards, evaluating school and student academic performance over time, and rewarding students, teachers, and schools for achievement gains.

The concept of an output-driven system as a means for reforming American schools was developed by James S. Coleman while he was a Fulbright Senior Scholar at the European University Institute in 1993. Having recently completed his major theoretical statement on sociology, *Foundations of Social Theory* (1990), Coleman returned to one of his primary interests in education; that is, how to form social norms in schools that could enhance student social development and improve academic performance. Reflecting on years of studying schools as social institutions, Coleman believed that strengthening the social ties among teachers and students would facilitate building norms that would motivate students to learn.

From Coleman's perspective, the relational ties among teachers and students in public elementary and secondary schools had become increasingly detached and indifferent to the point where teachers were often compromising their own professional standards in order to maintain social control in their classrooms. Instead of a classroom where teachers and students work toward a set of common performance goals, both parties often negotiate with each other to advance their own self interests-- students to get better grades for less effort, and teachers to achieve disciplinary compliance by assigning less homework and setting low standards for high grades.[1]

Coleman identified the problem of improving education as one of moving classrooms from an individual self-interest model to a model where norms extolling high performance were shared among teachers and students. Believing that the individual-interest model in many classrooms was antithetical to academic productivity, he began constructing a model for a new educational system that would transform the social context of the classroom in which teachers and students work. Coleman directed his efforts at creating incentive structures for schools and classrooms that would motivate teachers and students to support achievement norms and attain high levels of academic performance. This basic rationale guides the arguments and empirical analyses detailed in this book.

The Components of an Output-Driven System

Coleman's interest in education covered a wide range of topics. Over the years, he looked at the social status of adolescent peer groups (*Adolescent Society: Social Life of the Teenager and Its Impact on Education*, 1961), school factors that contribute to student achievement (*Equality of Educational Opportunity*, 1966), and relations between families, communities, and schools (*Public and Private Schools: The Impact of Communities*, 1987).[2] One area that was not investigated in these earlier studies was the relations among teachers and students and what effects the quality of these relations have on students' academic performance. In formulating the output-driven model, he focused on the heart of the educational enterprise, the interactions between teachers and students in classrooms.

These interactions do not occur in an isolated context. What occurs between teacher and student is influenced to a large extent by various layers of bureaucratic controls that surround and penetrate the classroom. Classrooms are nested within schools, schools within districts, and districts within states. Each of these layers of bureaucratic control has considerable authority to mandate policies that can either promote or be detrimental to the social and cognitive development of students.

The wide authority that individual districts or schools have to determine their own policies, often results in teachers being sent inconsistent and confusing messages about what constitutes acceptable levels of student performance. These sometimes conflicting and ambiguous expectations leave many teachers with the task of creating their own standards of classroom performance. Diverse standards of performance across classrooms make it extremely difficult to assure that students reach reasonable levels of achievement. However, externally based standards, Coleman asserted, could help to reshape the schooling system and create enabling conditions for enhancing classroom practices.

Coleman envisioned a single entity responsible for establishing standards for student and teacher performance that would operate independently of local school interests. External state standards boards could serve such a function providing they were free from partisan politics and the interests of local communities. By shifting the authority for standard setting and assessment to an independent external agency rather than an intermediary district, Coleman maintained, it would be easier to monitor and ensure compliance at the local level.

While standards should be set externally, he argued that the work in classrooms should be left to the discretion of the teacher. Instructional activities should center on trying to achieve the outcomes specified by external standards. Thus, local schools would retain autonomy over instructional methods, but the basic content of what should be taught and what students should know and be able to do would be dictated by external standards.

If an external agent acts as the standards setter and establishes a reliable program for student assessment, the basis for the teacher's authority in the classroom changes and the teacher has greater responsibility for ensuring that students achieve. In such a situation, the role of the teacher changes from evaluator to coach and facilitator. Changing the function of the teacher's role in the classroom to one of academic coach, Coleman argued, can help to establish new social norms about the value of learning.

But the teacher alone cannot set classroom norms. How learning is valued is shaped in part by the actions and attitudes of the students in the class and their parents. In many classrooms, especially in schools where community and family disorganization prevail, there is little if any reinforcement of school goals by community and family norms. The strong family and community norms which in the past had reinforced the school's goals have weakened, thus forcing many schools to function without the support that family and community once provided.

Many teachers have been forced to take on a more central responsibility in helping students learn. Instead of reinforcing family and community norms, teachers are often responsible for shaping student attitudes and commitments toward learning, including what they need to learn, how hard they should work, and how they should behave. This task is difficult in schools that have little family and community support for education. In these communities the teachers have little authority over their students. Therefore, it is clear that a new basis of authority and new methods for assuring its legitimacy are necessary for schools to succeed. Freeing teachers from being evaluators so they may become more focused on the instructional process is one way of altering the present authority structure in classrooms.

What the teacher believes, and consequently what she does and says in the classroom, rewards and sanctions certain responses of students or groups of students. For Coleman, such beliefs about what should be accomplished in the classroom are the primary mechanism for motivating student behaviors. By putting in place an incentive structure that rewards academic performance, classroom norms held by the teachers and students are more likely to change. To this end, Coleman outlined a series of incentives that would make teachers and students more enthusiastic participants in teaching and learning and more focused on achieving.

The incentive structure Coleman devised did not merely entail paying teachers more money or giving their classes special privileges such as taking field trips. For teachers, rewards for student achievement are based on a value added model. Instead of looking only at absolute levels of achievement, the focus is on the amount of progress a student has made during the school year. Thus, teachers are evaluated not only by the numbers of their students performing academically at grade level, but rather by the amount of progress individual students make during the academic year. Teachers who are able to advance the most deficient or most challenging students would receive extra compensation. Second, students who make the most relative progress would have greater choice in the educational market, that is, they would be given the first chance to select high quality schools and programs.

The output-driven model Coleman constructed should not be considered definitive in its approach. Rather, its elements can be linked to specific problems confronting educational systems. He did not imagine that his system would be readily adopted in full but had hoped that supporters and critics would see some mechanisms that could be introduced to facilitate school change. Among his major ideas were: to decentralize schools into smaller units, to involve parents in reviewing and deciding whether current school practices fit their child's educational needs, to implement new forms of assessment, and to make teachers accountable on the basis of how much each child had grown academically from one year to the next, taking into account the difficulties in raising the performance of students who begin with limited skills. To bring into the classroom a closer personal intimacy between the teacher and her/his class, he advocated that elementary teachers and students remain together over several years. Remaining with the same teacher has the advantage of reinforcing norms and building trust relationships among all those in the classroom.

Some might say that Coleman's ideas are not new, and many researchers and policymakers have advocated creating national or state standards as a key policy initiative aimed at increasing school quality (Smith and O'Day 1991; National Council for Education Standards and Testing 1992; McLaughlin and Shepard 1995). Requiring minimum competency examinations for high school graduation, frequent monitoring and reporting of student progress, and increasing course requirements for graduation are popular ways of raising curriculum standards and establishing accountability measures (Fuhrman 1993). Many local school systems have initiated policies designed to align specific curriculum objectives with instruction and student testing.

But what is new, and what is decidedly "Coleman-like," is his explicit focus on the importance of building positive social relationships between the teacher and the student around norms that stress academic achievement. Instituting standards or bringing in new programs alone often does little to change how schools work. Without strong social ties between the teacher and her/his class, Coleman believed that it would be nearly impossible to establish norms that place a strong value on academic achievement. Without such norms, students and teachers would continue to have unclear understandings of what was expected of them and what they needed to do to reach acceptable levels of performance. Further, such norms cannot be sustained without reinforcement through incentives. In this case, the incentive for the student is access to a higher quality learning experience. While the incentives for the teacher are a new definition of her/his role, the opportunity to select her/his students, and obtain monetary rewards through salary increments.

Understanding the importance of norms for improving achievement can be traced to Coleman's theoretical work on social capital (Coleman 1988).

To Coleman, norms are transmitted through networks of social ties. Through social networks information and values are channelled from one individual to another. The tighter and denser the network, the more likely that the same information and values will be shared. In such conditions sanctions are easier to impose because those in the network share the same norms. Thus, in Coleman's view, the classroom should become a close network where high achievement plays a dominant role.

Unquestionably for Coleman, the most important norms were those that valued achievement. To him the primary goal of education was preparing children with intellectual skills necessary to become productive members of society. While he understood the importance of psychological and social development as outcomes of an educational system, he felt they were secondary to achievement and had been given too much attention in the curriculum. Students would develop a greater sense of self-esteem and personal satisfaction if they had knowledge of complex ideas and advanced skills in mathematics, reading, and reasoning. In many ways, the output-driven model exemplifies his overriding interest in the development of intellectual skills.

Testing whether the components of an output-driven system would work in the U.S. was particularly problematic since there are no existing models, and creating one would require such a departure from the current system that opportunities for doing so seemed highly improbable. Although there were no operating output-driven systems to examine, various elements of the design could be found in some schools. For example, there are some practices in schools that focus on evaluating principals and teachers on the basis of student achievement and rewarding students on the basis of high academic performance.

Such school practices could be identified in the National Education Longitudinal Study of 1988-1994 (NELS:88-94). Though certainly not ideal for evaluative purposes, the NELS:88-94 data set nonetheless provides a comprehensive range of various school practices. Further, it provides sufficiently large school and student samples to study whether output-driven practices would have a measurable impact on student performance when taking into account differences in student background factors.

To take advantage of the potential contained in the base year, first, and second follow-up of NELS:88-94, Coleman assembled a team of advanced graduate students at The University of Chicago to systematically investigate whether components of an output-driven system made a difference in student achievement. Using NELS:88-94, each team member assessed the effectiveness of a component of the output-driven model. While each individual had major responsibility for one aspect of the analyses, all research plans, empirical analyses and written reports were extensively reviewed by the entire team. For purposes of attribution, the author(s) who took primary responsibility for each chapter are identified.

Data Base and Sample Selection

The NELS:88-94 began in 1988 with a national representative sample of over 24,000 eighth graders and their parents, teachers, and school administrators. The students were followed as they made the transition from eighth grade to high school and on to postsecondary education and into the labor force. The empirical analyses in this book rely on the first and second follow-ups when the students were sophomores and seniors respectively.

Conducted by the National Center for Education Statistics (NCES), NELS:88-94 is the third in a series of national longitudinal studies of American students. The two earlier longitudinal studies sponsored by NCES include, the National Longitudinal Study of the High School Class of 1972 (NLS-72) and High School and Beyond (HS&B). Several of the chapters in this book refer to HS&B and one of the empirical analyses directly compares the mathematical performance of NELS:88-94 sophomores with HS&B sophomores.

Substantively, NELS:88-94 was designed to examine policy relevant information concerning the effectiveness of schools, curricular offerings, course taking behaviors, variations in curricular content, and instructional techniques in mathematics, science, reading and social studies. Most of the analytical work in this book focuses on students' experiences in high school, including information on participation in classes and extra curricular activities, work outside of school, educational expectations, occupational aspirations, preparation for college admissions, and relationships with family and friends. Several of the analyses draw upon information about the high school from the school administrator study, and family background information from the parent questionnaire given in the base year and second follow-up. One analysis also uses information from the mathematics and science teacher questionnaires given at the first follow-up. Each chapter provides a full description of the variables and the surveys from which they were obtained.

A few words need to be said about the NELS:88-94 elementary and high school samples and student samples. Unlike HS&B, the first student sample was drawn when the students were in eighth grade. Although there was a representative sample of elementary schools in the eighth grade, when the students went on to high school the school sample was no longer a representative sample of high schools. Because of this factor, our focus is on the students and what practices at both the school and classroom level impact her/his academic achievement.

Generalizing about the student sample is possible because of weighting and freshening techniques (see the National Education Longitudinal Study of 1988-94 Sampling Design, Weighting and Estimation Report [Ingels, Scott and Frankel 1996] for further detail on this point). The base year sample of NELS was a clustered, stratified national probability sample of 1,052 public and private eighth grade schools. In spring of 1990 when most of these students were sophomores, they were sampled again. Many of the students in the eighth grade had entered high schools where they were the only student participating in NELS:88. A subsampling was therefore carried out proportional to the number of base year sampled students within a school, thus reducing the number of schools and students involved within the study. In 1990, a freshened sample was added to the first follow-up student component achieving a representative sample of the nation's sophomores. The second follow-up to NELS:88-94 began in 1992 when most sample members were seniors. A second freshened sample was again included to achieve a representative sample of the nation's seniors.

Weighting survey data compensates for unequal probabilities of selection and adjusts for the effects of nonresponse. We have used student weights in our analytical work to adjust for selection and nonresponse effects. Weighting formulae can be found in Ingels, Scott and Frankel (1996).

Organization of the Book

Chapter Two describes Coleman's principles of design for reforming schools. Several earlier versions of this work were given at different education and sociology workshops at The University of Chicago, and drafts of this work were circulated as unpublished manuscripts. A presentation on the topic was also made in spring of 1994 at the University of Notre Dame and appears as a chapter in *Restructuring Schools, Promising Practices and Policies*, edited by Maureen Hallinan (1995). The chapter in the Hallinan volume presents some material similar to what is contained in this chapter. However, this version presents the argument in full, providing a more complete elaboration of the design principles.

Chapter Three, by Huayin Wang, Kathryn S. Schiller, and Stephen Plank, examines the importance between family educational attainment and student test scores. In the early stages of the analyses, Coleman suspected that the achievement of students over time would be relatively flat or would dip slightly based on evidence from declines in the Scholastic

Aptitude Test (SAT) taken by students expecting to enroll in post secondary institutions and the relatively low performance of American students on international tests. He imagined that if one compared the trends of achievement using national longitudinal samples at two different time points one would find that today's high school sophomore students were not performing as well as students in the 1980's.

However, comparisons between sophomores' mathematical achievement in HS&B and sophomore mathematical performance on NELS:88 showed that students in 1990 were doing better than students in 1980. But the test score differences between 1980 and 1990 were not large and, some might say a little disappointing given the massive efforts at school reform. Others, however, might conclude that given the increasing diversity among American high school students the results are heartening.

But of even greater importance was that the improvement of NELS:88-94 students could be linked to the rising educational levels of their parents compared to the educational attainment levels of the HS&B students' parents. This result was most pronounced for African American students. Having parents who completed more education after high school graduation resulted in higher levels of achievement as compared to students with similar characteristics whose parents did not continue their education past high school.

Schooling and educational attainment matters for all students and perhaps especially for minorities. The relationship between family educational attainment and achievement reinforces the influence of family in promoting student academic performance. School reform initiatives that fail to recognize the role of families in the educational process are unlikely to succeed. In Coleman's output-driven model, the role of family is seen as important on two levels. First, he advocates that families need to reinforce school learning goals at home. But even more importantly, Coleman believed that families needed to be actively involved in choosing the best educational environment for their child. Thus, a major parental responsibility in the education process was deciding which school one's child should attend and monitoring the child's performance in that school.

Chapter 4, by Roger Shouse, ties the concept of output-driven schooling to that of academic press, that is, the extent to which a school's organizational culture is driven by academic values, incentives, and norms. By highlighting their academic mission, schools can distinguish themselves as institutions, thus ultimately producing higher achievement levels. In contrast to this idea of academic press, some schools lean more toward serving a social mission; that is toward promoting friendly and cohesive social relations among their students and adult members. Though improving students' academic performance may be viewed positively in such schools, building a strong sense of community often becomes the ultimate institutional goal.

In developing measures of academic press and sense of community, Shouse's analysis indicates the critical impact of academic press on student achievement. This achievement effect is especially strong for students in schools where the majority of students have families with poverty-level income and low levels of educational attainment. Shouse reports a negative association between a strong sense of community and achievement in such schools with deficient levels of academic press.

Most important, however, is Shouse's finding of how academic press and sense of community work together to produce strong achievement in low socioeconomic schools. It would appear that when schools pursue academic endeavors, cohesive social relations serve to amplify these understandings throughout the organization. He argues that such relations are a product of output-driven schools, the result of students and teachers working together to overcome common obstacles to meet common goals.

Chapter 5, by Stephen Plank, Huayin Wang, and Barbara Schneider, examines the relationship between several measures of output-driven school organization and student achievement in mathematics and science. The two main issues addressed are: (1) whether there are effects of a school's reliance on, and attention to, external standards on student achievement, and (2) whether these effects operate partially through specific teaching practices. This analysis elaborates upon the discussion in Chapter 2 pertaining to why output-driven organizational features should affect achievement, both directly and indirectly, via changed teaching practices and interpersonal dynamics in the classroom.

The specific output-driven measures that are investigated include; the relative influence of a student's test performance on the principal's evaluation, the frequency with which test results are sent to parents, teachers' control over curricular content and teaching techniques, the relative importance of absolute achievement in determining students' grades, and the relative importance of individual improvement in determining students' grades. Among the noteworthy findings are the positive effects of sending test results to parents, and of teachers' reliance on absolute achievement when determining students' grades. Also, there is evidence that it is beneficial to achievement to limit the control teachers have over curricular content while granting teachers a high level of autonomy in determining teaching techniques.

Based upon the final models, the following interpretation is made regarding the control of content and teaching techniques: placing control of curricular content outside of the teacher's discretion is desirable because it enhances the probability that topics will be taught sequentially from year to year and lessens the chance that key curricular topics will not be covered. Moving curricular control to a more central authority can be beneficial to the teachers. Such an organizational change can help teachers focus on their teaching techniques, fine-tune their styles and structure their classroom environments to suit their students. Consistent evidence is shown with the claim that when teachers have the freedom to fine-tune and customize teaching techniques, they are able to inspire students to behave well and work hard. This good behavior and hard work, in turn, are associated with high achievement.

One important component of the output-driven model is the use of external examinations as a means for motivating both teachers and students to work toward a common goal of high academic achievement. Chapter 6, by Kathryn S. Schiller, explores the effect of the most common external examination in the U.S., the SAT, on the achievement growth of high school students. This analysis shows that sophomores who reported planning to take the SAT had higher growth rates in their mathematics tests by the time they were seniors than sophomores who did not have those plans. The effect of planning to take the SAT remains strong even when taking into account students' social backgrounds, success in school, and educational expectations.

However, planning to take the SAT did not have the same effect on achievement for all groups of students. The increases in mathematics achievement were generally highest among those students for whom college attendance may be problematic, such as those whose grades were borderline for college admission in competitive institutions or who have not taken college preparatory mathematics courses. This suggests that the SAT acts as an incentive for mathematics achievement for those students mentioned above and not others, such as those with extremely strong or weak academic records.

Based on these results, it would seem that one must take into account students' goals, their access to information and their academic preparedness, when designing incentive systems based on external examinations. The incentive system will not motivate students if they: are not aware of the examination, do not see doing well on it as important or requiring effort, or feel it is not a legitimate assessment of their achievements. This means that the external examination must be carefully designed to be fair to all groups along with being widely publicized and based on high standards, attainment of which is tied to clear consequences for students' lives. As a key part of an output-driven system, such examinations would help students and teachers focus their team efforts on reaching those high standards and gaining rewards for doing so.

The final chapter, by Barbara Schneider, attempts to show aspects of the output-driven model that could be implemented in the schools. Several principles of the output-driven model are already in place. For example, in a new project at Johns Hopkins University's Center for Social Organization of Schools, researchers from Johns Hopkins University and Howard University have been experimenting with changing the role of the teacher to one that is more coach-like rather than as a traditional evaluator. In this final chapter we identify some of these reform efforts and project which parts of the output-model seem most well-suited to bring about educational change.

Notes

1. Coleman's views of the unequal exchange process of teacher awarded grades for student effort was not based on conjecture. Extensive empirical analyses of this exchange process, first described in *Foundations of Social Theory* (1990), failed to demonstrate with large samples that students were motivated to work hard for higher grades. This was the case even for students who tended to receive high grades. This suggests that something else was being exchanged, such as good behavior for grades.

2. This is not meant to be an exhaustive list of Coleman's work in education but an attempt to highlight some of his major publications and areas of concern. For a more comprehensive analysis of Coleman's work see Clark (1996).

2

Output-Driven Schools: Principles of Design

James S. Coleman

Schools and school systems are organizations constructed for a purpose. In this, they stand in contrast to primordial organizations like the family. Although early schools had close links to family and community, modern schools increasingly have come to resemble other constructed organizations, such as business firms, which are bureaucratic in form. Schools share with other constructed organizations the characteristic that their design may be evaluated by the organization's efficiency in achieving its purpose.

Classical bureaucratic theory provided the guidelines for many early forms of constructed organizations. Schools and school systems soon followed suit, adopting this bureaucratic form, with authority residing at the top and delegated down through an administrative hierarchy. More recently, many constructed organizations have taken new directions which are distinctively different from classic bureaucratic design and practice.

This chapter describes new directions taken by some constructed organizations, sketches the outline of a theory which characterizes them, and examines the theory's applicability to schools. The end result is an organizational design that deviates sharply from that found in most schools in this country. Implicit in this design is the contention that the productivity of schools depends primarily on their organizational design. With the appropriate structure, the elements necessary for high productivity fall into place.

Innovations in Organizations

Max Weber was one of the first sociologists to attempt to develop a theory for non-primordial constructed organizations (Weber 1947). He described such organizations as "rational authority systems" and specified their characteristics, with the ideal type being the bureaucratic form. This form, with variations, has been the widespread paradigm upon which the rationalization of modern society has proceeded. However, in recent years, many business firms have initiated new organizational practices, some of which have little in common with the theory and practice of bureaucratic authority as described by Weber.

One of the first deviations from the classic bureaucratic model was the development of the multidivisional firm, initiated by General Motors in the l930s, and described by Chandler (1962). This structure gave both more autonomy and accountability to the firm's divisions. Relative autonomy of divisions was introduced in this structure, along with internal pricing of goods and services produced and consumed by divisions. This, in effect, made each division a profit center. Specifically, General Motors gave end product divisions the right to buy parts from outside suppliers rather than in-house parts producers, and it gave parts producers the right to sell their products to customers outside the firm.

Another innovation, one which goes beyond the multidivisional firm, is franchising. Franchising, which has recently become widespread, takes various forms. These forms have in common a contractual relation between the central franchising organization and the franchisee (usually a retailer), with a portion of the income going to the franchiser and a portion to the franchisee.

Some organizations have developed a modus operandi which involves the funding of spinoffs by employees who develop a potentially profitable product idea. The spinoff is a joint venture between the parent firm and the person or persons who developed the idea. One of the earliest firms to engage in this activity was 3M of Minneapolis, which saw itself as a central bank and research and development center to finance ideas generated by employees, particularly those engaged in research and development. Other similar organizational innovations can be found in the computer hardware and software industries, as well as in genetic engineering firms. The latter involve creative arrangements between university faculty members and biotechnical firms to establish either independent startups or spinoffs.

Rights, Responsibilities, and Incentives

From the relatively mature automobile industry has arisen an innovation which can be described as a reallocation of rights. This innovation began with Japanese firms and several variations can be found in American firms. One major component of this innovation is the right to reject parts or stop the production line. In the classic manufacturing organization, the supervisor or foreman in an assembly line does not have the right to reject input parts that are out-of-specification. He or she may only have the right to request from a higher supervisor in the plant that the parts be rejected. The decision to reject typically depends on whether it is possible to work around the defect without shutting down the assembly line. When a defect that can be repaired is found that can be repaired, a tag is put on the car, and at the end of the line, all cars with tags on them are shunted to a repair facility. Whether the line is shut down or not, the right to make that decision is never in the hands of the assembly line worker. Instead, this right is granted only to the line foreman or a superior of the line foreman.

In the Japanese auto assembly line, this right is allocated somewhat differently. The right to reject out-of-specification inputs, including the right to shut down the line, is held by the individual worker on the line who must use these parts in accomplishing the task. Workers are motivated to reject out-of-specification parts, because they are responsible for the quality of the component part as it moves to the next stage of the assembly line. Therefore, the right to reject input parts is accompanied by the responsibility for the output being *in* specification. As a result, the worker has an incentive not to accept input parts that are out-of-specification, as well as to insure that labor input does not result in an out-of-specification output.

The general character of the incentive that is introduced by this change in rights is fairly obvious. There is now an incentive for the worker to inspect the input parts and to be careful about possible production flaws introduced during processing. The set of rights that is involved in building automobiles is a string of rights which mirrors the production process itself. The workers who receive worker A's output have the right to reject worker A's production. The holders of the ultimate right to reject, however, are outside the organization altogether. The shipper, the dealer, and the customer can each reject the finished product.

Along with these rights is the workers' right to extra pay, depending on the quality and quantity of the output produced by the work group. When the work group rejects worker A's output, they are affecting A's pay, which is partially based on bonuses. This action may also affect the pay of others in the same work group as A. This incentive of extra pay serves to monitor and sanction the responsibilities of each work group. But, more importantly, it also provides a lever to increase the total efficiency of the production process.

This allocation of rights and responsibilities produces what may be described as an output-driven structure, in which the required quality of the product at one stage drives the performance at the preceding stage, all the way back through the production process of the organization. The feedback loop from the production of a defect to the discovery of the defect and then back to the producer of the defect is extremely short. This contrasts sharply with the long feedback loop that is characteristic of classical bureaucratic structures.

Organizations that are structured with short feedback loops are more characteristic of those which I term output-driven, whereas organizations with long feedback loops can be described as administratively-driven. In contrast to the Japanese automotive plant, which can be described as output-driven, a large, hierarchically structured, centralized school system would be a prime example of an administratively-driven organization. Figure 2.1 illustrates these two structures.

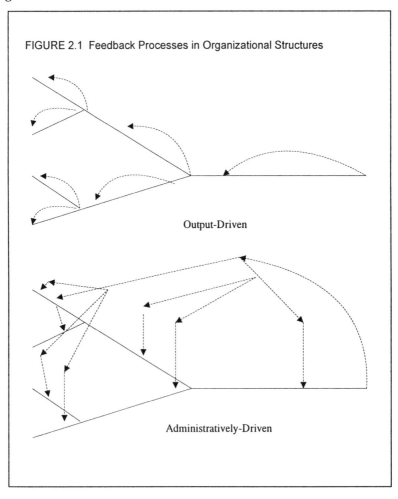

FIGURE 2.1 Feedback Processes in Organizational Structures

Output-Driven

Administratively-Driven

Another distinguishing feature of the Japanese plant concerns who has the right to exercise authority in the production process. In the classic bureaucratic structure, this right is held by a foreman. In the Japanese plant, this reallocated right is held collectively by the members of the assembly or subassembly line, called a Quality Circle. This collectivity has three distinctive rights. First, it has the right to reject the partially completed auto which it received from the preceding line. Second, it has the right to reorganize its own production process. Finally, the collectivity, rather than an individual, has the right to exercise extensive authority over its members. The foreman position is nonexistent in the firm's structure.

The rights held by the Quality Circle, together with the fact that members' bonuses depend on the group's quality of production, encourage norms that are consistent with and reinforce the organization's goals. For this to occur, it is important that the group not be too large. Quality Circles, for example, typically have 8 to 12 members.

The importance of small manageable groups needs to be underscored. In large groups it is difficult for individuals to communicate with one another on a consistent basis. The lack of communication makes it difficult to monitor work group production. But, more importantly, it undermines efforts at maintaining productivity-oriented norms. Mackie (1991) concluded from his study of cooperative work groups employed to plant trees under contract to the U.S. Forest Service that 12 members was an optimum size for a work group. There was nothing magical about the number 12 as an optimal size for a cooperative work group. Although Mackie describes this as an optimal size, it is not clear that 15 or 8 may not be better, depending on the nature of the task. All the innovations that I have described can be seen as attempts to overcome the incentive problems that arise in a centrally directed, hierarchically structured organization. By making benefits (i.e., income, autonomy, and responsibility) contingent on the quality and quantity of what is produced, the organization creates a direct link between effort and reward. In the multidivisional firm, the link is at the divisional level, in franchising it is at the franchise owner level, and in spinoff joint ventures it is at the entrepreneur level. In firms with Quality Circles, it is at the work group level.

In the case of Quality Circles, and very likely in the others as well, this organizational innovation does more than overcome the incentive problems often found in hierarchical organizations, where wage benefits get determined according to piecework pay rates. The Quality Circle creates a social group in whose interest it is to encourage high effort and careful work from its members. The social norms in the Quality Circle come into being to reinforce organizational goals. These norms go beyond overcoming the incentive problems of hierarchical organizations. They provide extra incentives of their own, because each member's work benefits all. This comes about because rights, which in the hierarchical organization are held centrally and delegated vertically, are decentralized and given to subgroups--divisions, franchisees, and Quality Circles.

The allocation of rights in these organizational innovations involves a fundamental redesign of the firm. The Weberian bureaucracy can be described as administratively-driven; these innovations create, to differing degrees, organizations that are output-driven. The degree to which the organization as a whole can be said to be output-driven depends on the extent to which rewards and sanctions are based on external criteria that are shared among the subgroups, such as the Quality Circles. In the case of the automotive firm, the external criteria would be producing a high quality product.

School Design

From the organizational innovations previously discussed, two elements are especially applicable for the redesign of American schools. The first of these elements is the replacement of the administratively-driven organization by one that is output-driven and is characterized by small autonomous groups that have specific rights and can exercise authority over their members. The second element is the explicit creation of social capital in the organizational design. Social capital, which is the relational tie among members of a social system accumulated for productive ends, serves an important role in maintaining social norms (Coleman 1988, 1990).

In the instance of the Quality Circles in Japanese automobile manufacturing firms, social capital is brought about primarily by the allocation of rights and obligations not merely to individual positions in the organization, but also to subgroups in the organization. These subgroups, which are not hierarchically organized from without, can create their own internal structure. The subgroups must be small enough and have sufficiently dense interactions to be norm generating bodies. If rights are allocated appropriately, norms will arise that support and reinforce the goals of the organization. If rights are allocated inappropriately, the norms that arise will act against the organization's goals.

Diagnosis of American Education

With these organizational innovations in mind, let us now turn to the question of how schools might be modified to improve their functioning. It is useful to begin with a diagnosis of American education. Since there are a number of dimensions along which children develop during their formative years, the schools have multiple goals, such as educational achievement and social development. There is, however, a justification for laying out a design for schools which focuses on one goal. When an educational system is seriously deficient with respect to an important goal, then it is reasonable to carry out designs which specifically attend to that goal.

Clearly, academic achievement is one of the major production goals of the educational system. This goal, I contend, is seriously deficient in most educational systems in the U.S. Relative to students in other industrial countries, American students have for some time scored at or near the bottom on standardized tests (Husen 1967). Measures of performance both before and after the test score decline of the 1970s continue to show that many American adolescents graduate from high school with limited basic skills in reading and mathematics. This is the case throughout all grade levels.

The ineffectiveness of inner city schools is well known, and the weak performance of the children who attend them is extensively documented. This weak performance is found in all types of communities, that is, rural and suburban, as well as urban. For example, Bishop (1991) notes that "the gap between American high school seniors in middle class suburbs and their counterparts in many northern European countries and Japan is larger than the two to three grade level equivalent gap between whites and blacks in the U.S."

Looking at the distribution of scores, the low levels of performance of American students at the high end of the test score scale are ordinarily overlooked. But, the well-known Scholastic Aptitude Test (SAT) score decline of the 1970s and 1980s shows the greatest loss among students who score at the top end of the test score distribution (Murray and Hernstein 1992).

Another example of the low levels of performance can be found in Minneapolis, Minnesota, where students tend to score near the top on standardized tests compared to other American students. Here student performance in 20 fifth grade mathematics classrooms was compared with the performance of fifth graders in 20 classrooms in Taipei, Taiwan, and in Sendai, Japan. The average for the highest performing classroom in Minneapolis was below that for even the lowest performing classroom in Sendai. It was also below that for 19 of the 20 classrooms in Taipei (Stevenson et al. 1985; Stevenson, Lee and Stigler 1986). Mathematics is not the only area where American students score below students in other countries. The performance of Americans in foreign languages is also low in comparison with students in other industrialized countries. Furthermore, American students study foreign languages at a much lower rate, and only one state requires foreign language study for high school graduation (Willis 1996).

The long term implications of Americans' poor academic performance can be seen in many institutions of higher education in this country. For example, in 1991 one-fifth of the mathematics doctoral holders in the U.S. labor force were foreign-born (NSF 1994). Moreover, of the 1,226 new doctoral mathematics recipients in the U.S in 1994-95, 627 of the 1,124 for whom citizenship status was known were non-U.S. citizens (Fulton 1995). It would appear that American scientific and technological achievements are becoming increasingly dependent on a "brain drain" from countries outside the U.S. I would argue that if another country were to become a more attractive destination for these immigrants, so that we had to depend on our own educational system for producing scientists, we could not maintain our current technological levels, much less innovate technologically.

The low level of academic performance in American schools is reinforced by yet another aspect of most schools. In middle schools and high schools, across the socioeconomic spectrum and among all racial and ethnic groups, the informal norms that develop among students are not norms that extol achievement. Rather, they are norms that scorn effort, and reward scholastic achievement only when it appears to be done without effort. Anti-achievement norms need not predominate, and there are some high schools in which they do not. But, I would suggest that there are more schools in some countries outside the U.S. where high achievement norms predominate. It is a mark of inadequate organizational design that these anti-achievement norms exist in schools.

The sources of the low effort put into high achievement are several, but one is especially important: the lack of well-publicized external criteria of performance from which meaningful consequences flow. In the absence of such criteria, there can develop an implicit compact to reduce demands imposed by high standards, such as the assignment of extensive homework, and the parents' inabilities and unwillingness to make their children complete their homework. This implicit compact can result in low levels of performance. An example can be seen in an incident reported by Arthur Powell in a high school he visited:

> Students were given time [in class] to read *The Scarlet Letter*, *The Red Badge of Courage*, *Huckleberry Finn*, and *The Great Gatsby* because they would not read the books if they were assigned as homework. Parents had complained that such homework was excessive. Pressure from them might even bring the teaching of the books to a halt...(as one teacher put it) "If you can't get them to read at home,

you do the next best thing. It has to be done...I'm trying to be optimistic and say we're building up their expectations in school" (Powell, Farrar and Cohen 1985, 81).

Another example of this implicit compact which undermines high achievement norms is reported by Theodore Sizer in describing one teacher's class:

> He signaled to the students what the minimum, the few questions for a test, were; all tenth and eleventh graders could master these with absurdly little difficulty. The youngsters picked up the signal and kept their part of the bargain by being friendly and orderly. They did not push Brady, and he did not push them...Brady's room was quiet, and his students liked him. No wonder he had the esteem of the principal who valued orderliness and good rapport between students and staff. Brady and his class had agreement all right, agreement that reduced the efforts of both student and teacher to an irreducible and pathetic minimum (Sizer 1984, 156).

How can a teacher gain the friendly and orderly classroom climate that Brady has and at the same time the kind of effort and involvement that generates high achievement? The teacher faces a dilemma; he or she must either impose high standards and sacrifice friendly relations, risking a rebellion, or lower the standards and sacrifice achievement. One of the solutions to this dilemma, in the absence of strong parental demands that can hold a rebellion in check, is for the teacher to be freed from the task of setting the standards. Then the teacher and the class can engage in a common task, that of attaining the externally established standards. Standards may consist of an external test, contests with students in other schools, or perhaps other activities. The crucial element is that the standards are out of the teacher's control. The teacher and the students share a common interest which generates both the effort needed for achievement and a positive climate.

There was an interesting "natural experiment" involving the absence of any external demands whatsoever toward school learning. An Englishman, A.S. Neill, established a boarding school, Summerhill, in which no external demands were made upon the children; there were no classes, no assignments, and no school. According to accounts of Summerhill by Neill and others, it was a very pleasant place, one in which the children managed their own affairs individually and collectively, but as Neill himself put it, one in which "the children of Summerhill were not much interested in book learning" (Neill 1960).

There is one exception to the lack of external demands at Summerhill. When the children reached their upper teens, they saw that in order to manage in the outside world, they would need a school leaving certificate, which required passing a set of externally imposed examinations. Thus, in their last year at Summerhill, they spent a considerable amount of time studying, in order to pass these examinations. This last-year studying is the exception that proves the rule: When an external criterion is imposed, efforts toward learning begin.

A much cruder and more partial natural experiment can be found in the comparison between American and Japanese schools. In Japanese schools, where there are strong externally imposed standards, the achievement is much higher than in American schools. In Japan, however, there is lower satisfaction with the schools, and parents are less satisfied with their children's performance than are parents in the U.S. This is sometimes seen as paradoxical; American children learn much less than students in Japan, but they and their parents are more content with their educational performance (Stevenson, Chen and Lee 1993). But, as in the description of Brady's classroom, American children are content, because they are satisfying the demands made on them. These demands are minimal, because the majority of students are unwilling to meet stronger ones.

Just like adults, adolescents have a time-and-attention budget. Over the years the amount of time budgeted for doing homework has declined to about 3-1/2 hours per week, half of what it was in the 1970s before the SAT test score decline. Sports, part-time jobs, and television all compete with homework for the teenager's time. As the time spent on homework has declined, the time spent in part-time jobs (about 10 hours a week for high school seniors, see Snyder and Hoffman 1995) and in watching television has increased. At 20 hours per week, American teenagers spend two to three times as much time watching television in comparison to students in other Organization for Economic Cooperation and Development (OECD) countries (Hewlett 1991).

Clearly, since the 1960s, other activities, such as television viewing and earning money at part-time jobs, have come to occupy a more important place in the average teenager's life than homework. Parents appear unable to change this. One of the major obstacles to reallocating youngsters' time can be traced to the social organization of many American elementary and secondary schools.

Administratively-Driven Versus Output-Driven Schools

Schools as they exist in the U.S. are neither purely administratively- nor output-driven. Most schools, however, are hierarchical systems, with the building principal as the immediate authority. Principals, in turn, report to the school district superintendent, who is the central authority. Principals often have little discretionary authority over resources, hiring of teachers, and other decisions. Thus, in contrast to the organizations that have adopted innovations which decentralize authority, most school structures remain clear examples of bureaucratic, administratively-driven organizations.

However, when output-driven designs are used in educational systems they can be very powerful. For example, college entrance requirements in the U.S. have usually required 32 "Carnegie units" of high school courses, including such specific requirements as two years of a foreign language. Traditionally, these entrance requirements have dictated the college preparatory curriculum in high schools. In the 1960s and 70s, colleges liberalized their entrance requirements, partially in response to the youth revolt and the civil rights movement (Boyer 1987). Most elite colleges dropped their foreign language entrance requirement, and consequently, foreign language course taking in high schools dropped precipitously. Only in the late 1980s, when colleges reinstated the language requirement, were foreign language courses in high schools revived. It is important to note that the external demand imposes requirements not upon output, but upon actions. The Carnegie-unit example illustrates how relaxation of a demand can have negative effects.

There are other examples, and an interesting one is handwriting. High schools, as the recipients of the products of middle schools, set the external requirements for middle schools, and middle schools set the external requirements for elementary schools. When high school teachers no longer required good handwriting, middle school teachers did not either. When this occurred, elementary school teachers stopped teaching children to have good handwriting.

Despite their hierarchical authority structure, educational systems are partially output-driven, as these examples indicate. The presence of some output-driven elements in a system that is predominately administratively-driven places teachers in an untenable position. Teachers are constrained to meet certain output demands, yet they are subject to authority which eliminates their autonomy in meeting these demands. The qualities of the output-driven model infused into the system are defective, in that they exist only in a partial form. Without external standards of performance which students are expected to achieve, the students and teachers are not actually held accountable for their activities. In the absence of external standards, teachers set flexible internal standards, as in the case of Mr. Brady's class, which have negative repercussions.

The absence of external standards for performance has several negative consequences. Teachers are put in the position of establishing the requirements, by having to decide what levels of performance will be necessary for the awarding of a given grade. The teacher has two roles with conflicting interests: as the person who sets the standards, and as the person who tries to get students to meet the standards. This creates an ambivalent relationship between teacher and students, quite different from that commonly found between coach and performers. The coach can devote her/his undivided efforts to improving the performance of the team members, while the teacher's efforts must be on two fronts. He or she must improve students' performance, and struggle with students over the level of performance required for a given grade. This can weaken student-teacher relations, voiding the effort toward students' performance. The teacher's divided effort is also a counterproductive element, because it contributes to anti-achievement norms among students which restrict their output. Students would have fewer reasons to develop such anti-achievement norms if the standards used to measure performance were not under the teacher's control.

Another negative consequence of the absence of external standards is the creation of an incentive for a student to take easy courses. A student's grade point average (GPA) creates a rank in class, which is well-known by students and widely used for college admission. But, a student's GPA can be augmented with less effort and greater certainty by taking easy courses, rather than by performing well in difficult courses. Various devices have been introduced to signal to colleges that grades are based on hard or easy courses, but none of this would be necessary if class rank were not based on teacher-established standards in specific courses, but on externally established standards in specific areas of performance.

A third defect of internally established standards is that they introduce noise into the information the receiving institution (in the case of the high school graduate, the postsecondary institution or employer) gets from the school regarding the student's performance. Employers seldom use test scores or transcripts in hiring, and when colleges make admission decisions, they often augment class rank information with scores on the SAT or the American College Test (ACT), and sometimes even with the ranking of the school itself. This would not be necessary if standards were set externally rather than internally, because students from all schools would be assessed on a uniform set of standards.

One major rationale for schools' use of internal standards of achievement, rather than externally established ones, is the great disparity in the performance of students from different backgrounds and with different preparation. The use of internal standards, even taking these factors into consideration, is not an effective way for assessing and rewarding student performance.

In approaching the design of schools as organizations, several concepts are useful. Although I have used some of these concepts earlier in the chapter, it would be beneficial to list them and provide brief definitions here.

A Set of Definitions

Output-driven: An organizational form in which the rewards and punishments for performance in productive activity come from the recipient of the product. Applied to intermediate products within the organization, this means that the recipient of the intermediate product has the right to monitor the quality of that product, and, thus, to determine the rewards and punishments for the part of the organization from which it receives intermediate products--and, in turn, the obligation to satisfy the requirements that its own products must meet--as monitored by the recipients of *its* products.

Administratively-driven: An organizational form in which the rewards and punishments for performance in productive activity come from the central authority in a hierarchical structure, through an immediate supervisor.

External standards: Standards that are set outside the organization, ordinarily by the recipient of the product of the organization.

Stages of schooling: elementary school (grades 1-4; ages 6-9), middle school (grades 5-8; ages 10-13), high school (grades 9-12; ages 14-17).

Value added or performance gain: These two terms will be used interchangeably. They mean the difference in the performance level at the end of one stage of schooling and the performance level at the end of the prior stage. The terms are also used to refer to yearly differences in performance levels.

Rights allocation: The allocation of rights in the organization by the central authority to positions in or subdivisions of the organization.

Incentive: Any source of motivation to apply effort toward a goal. Here the term is applied to teachers, students, and parents.

Informal norms: This term is used to apply to norms that arise within an organization, and which are held by all or some of its members. The norms may be facilitated through structures established by design, or they may be unanticipated and unintended by the organization's designer. Informal norms held by the teachers in a school and informal norms held by students in the school are discussed separately.

Social capital: This term refers to the informal social relations, primordial institutions (families, religious groups), and other informal institutions that exist in the environments of the children in a school, insofar as they can serve to augment the education of the children. It is also used to refer to social relations and norms that arise spontaneously within a constructed organization, when these augment the organization's goals.

School: A set of 4-16 non-specialist teachers with primary responsibility for a set of children at the elementary, middle, or high school level. In addition to the teachers, the school includes a building and a building custodian. The internal organization of the teachers is up to them. They may decide, for example, that one among them is to be "head teacher" or "principal."

Specialist: This term refers to a teacher, who, under contract with the non-specialist teachers in schools, teaches or coaches students from more than one school in non-core special areas. These include music, drama, other performing arts, and advanced topics in mathematics, sciences, sports, technical skills, and other areas.

Designing an Output-Driven System

To design an output-driven system, it is important to begin at the end and work backwards. This necessity arises, because the standards at the final output, when properly employed, provide the motivating factor that reverberates back through each of the earlier stages to energize and focus actions. What is imperative, then, is a reward for performance at the end of the process of elementary and secondary education. It cannot, however, be a reward which comes only to teachers, or only to the students, or only to their parents. There are three parties whose actions are directly relevant to achievement: the child, the parent, and the teacher. High achievement requires that each of these three parties must be motivated to bring it to fruition.

The evaluation system on the basis of which teachers, students, and parents are rewarded must contain several requirements that must be met.

I.   *The standards must be externally designed and externally administered by those parties that will be the institutions receiving the "graduates" of the school.*

Comment: For the high school, there are two such tests for college admission, the SAT and the ACT. There are no such tests for high school graduates who will enter other institutions. However, for sports played in high school that are also collegiate sports, being selected to play on a team can act as a measurable evaluation system. Results from extensive interscholastic competitions allow high school students to exhibit their competence. In areas where interscholastic debate is widespread, the same is true to a lesser extent for debaters. In those states which have statewide interscholastic competitions in music, drama, and other areas, there is the basis for such an evaluation system in these areas as well. Advanced Placement tests provide a starting point for such evaluation in particular academic areas.

There are international "olympics" at the high school level in some specialized technical areas, in which students from some countries participate. There is also an academic olympics, at least in the fields of mathematics, in which some countries, including the U.S. participate. Thus, in many specialized areas, there already exists the basis for externally designed performance tests.

However, there exists little basis for externally designed standards for the end of middle school and the end of elementary school. Following the logic of output-driven organization, the design should come from, or at least be extensively informed by, teachers at the next level: high school teachers for the tests at the end of middle school, and middle school teachers for the tests at the end of elementary school. These tests, however, can hardly be designed without knowledge of what the criteria at the end of high school will be.

II.   *The system must evaluate not "basic abilities," but achievement.*

Comment: The SAT and ACT tests currently used in the U.S. for college admission fail this criterion. From the outset, the SAT was designed to be "curriculum-free," and students were told that it is not possible to study for the SAT. It is, in fact, possible to increase one's performance on the SAT; there are commercial organizations which provide courses that do so. But, the fiction was strongly maintained by the SAT test-makers at the Educational Testing Service, which constructs the SAT, until several studies and organizations proved that it was possible to improve performance substantially (Crouse and Trusheim 1988).

One original aim of the SAT was to give students from weaker high schools the same chance to score a good grade as students from stronger high schools. The effect, however, in contrast to English O- and A- levels, the French Baccalaureate, and the German Abitur, was to deprive the SAT of any motivating power toward achievement. In transmitting the notion that what is tested is immutable, the SAT and ACT tests are *less* egalitarian than a test which is explicitly tied to curriculum, because they create the belief that the score measures one's self, fixed and immutable, relative to others.

III. *The system must evaluate not only the performance **level**, but also the performance **gains** over the period between test administrations (a year, or a 4-year school).*

Comment: If an evaluation provides rewards only for level of achievement, there are at least two negative consequences. First, it leads only to interpersonal comparison (rather than to comparison with the student's own prior performance), which tends to differentially motivate persons who are at different points in the distribution of achievement. Only those at the high end of the distribution are highly motivated. Second, it can be seen as unfair to teachers, parents, and students. If we accept that different children have different abilities, then to measure all against a single standard of performance is not to have a level playing field. Different abilities give, in effect, differentially efficient equipment to students, parents, and teachers, to reach the same goal.

But, if an evaluation provides rewards only for gains in achievement, then there also are at least two negative consequences. One is that this creates a moral hazard: gains in achievement can be brought about not only by high final levels of achievement, but also by low initial levels of achievement. Thus, this creates a motivation to have low initial scores, as well as a motivation to have high final scores. Second, a system of evaluation that rewards only gains in achievement lacks the authenticity that one which rewards levels of achievement automatically carries. Having a set of standards against which the product of the system can be measured gives the evaluation system both legitimacy and stability. Thus, it would lack the legitimacy necessary for a stable evaluation system.

Not only do the evaluations used in the U.S., the SAT and the ACT, fail this criterion, but also the Baccalaureate, Abitur, and A- levels fail it, as well. Each measures level of performance, and, thus, serves its motivating function only for high performers; there is no measure of gain in performance.

IV. *The evaluation must provide rewards that motivate teachers, parents, and students.*

Comment: Certain evaluation systems, such as those in the Japanese and Hungarian systems, and to a lesser extent, those in various European countries, meet this criterion, despite failing others. The Hungarian system does this through contests at the local, regional, national, and international levels. Teachers gain prestige and the opportunity to move to a more prestigious school by having high-performing students, just as coaches do in the U.S. Students and parents are motivated to win the prize. The defect, of course, is that the effectiveness of this reward differs greatly at different points in the distribution of performance. It is most effective for high achievers, and for teachers and parents of high achievers.

Teachers can be motivated by pay, by career opportunities, and by autonomy in their jobs. Students and parents can be motivated by various benefits to be discussed, and also by recognition for doing well; but, recognition for doing well academically is not automatic.

Yet, recognition depends on conditions under the control of educational policy. For example, schools now have informal rankings in parents' and teachers' minds in terms of the *level* of performance of students. This is reinforced by the reporting of standardized test scores in local newspapers. But, if the year-to-year *gains* in performance (for example, gains in percentile position or standard score) were reported, there would be a shift in the rankings, as a consequence of the publication of the gains in scores.

Analytical Elements Necessary for an Output-Driven School

In the designs that I will lay out, there are six elements that are central, each of which is not present in the design of current schools for American children. I see these elements as necessary to the design of schools to be output-driven in the sense used in this chapter.

1. Externally imposed standards as the basis for all evaluations of student performance.

2. Evaluations based on two measures: *level* of performance, and *performance gain* or *value added*.

3. Yearly rewards to teachers, students, and parents for level of performance and performance gain.

4. Using the final output criteria (the externally imposed standards) as the starting point for designing evaluations at each stage of the education of a child, namely the creation of a system with short feedback loops.

5. Allocation of rights and responsibilities not only to individuals, but also to groups of teachers, groups of students, and groups of parents, to encourage the development of social capital, that is, informal norms that support educational goals.

6.   The use of a core of academic achievement plus areas of specialized performance (which may be academic, but need not be) as the performance criteria.

Possible Designs. With these as analytical points, it is useful to describe possible organizational designs. These designs incorporate the necessary elements described above, but are only examples of the many possible designs which contain these elements.

Design 1.

1.   At the end of high school, each student takes an externally designed and administered examination in academic subjects. A great deal of experience exists for this examination. The International Baccalaureate exists, and in most European countries, there are examples of academic achievement tests for a high school diploma. Each student would take a second test, in topics ranging from advanced mathematics to performing arts to technical skills to athletics. Upon leaving high school, the student would have a portfolio consisting of scores on each subject in the academic test, plus performance evidence in the specialized field, plus attendance and discipline. This portfolio is the graduate's credential for employers or higher education.

2.   A student receives a grade in each academic subject at the end of each year of each school, based on an externally designed examination. Two grades are given, one being the level of performance on the test, and the other being the value added, or performance gain, that is, the difference between the test score at the end of the previous year and the test score at the end of the current year.

3.   Value added at each of the three levels of school (elementary, middle, and secondary) is determined by the difference in performance between the end of the preceding level and the end of this level in academic subjects. Value added is determined separately for each child, but is a combined measurement across subject matters in the academic test given at the end of each school.

4.   The test at the end of each level is externally designed and externally administered. Teachers have full control over

preparation of their students, curriculum, and teaching methods, but not over the content of the examination their students will take, nor the conditions under which they take it. The areas of achievement covered by the examinations are made public to facilitate preparation for the examinations, as is true for the European end-of-secondary-school examinations.

5. The groups of teachers at each of the three school levels are rewarded each year with bonuses for the value added for each of the children who "graduate" from their responsibility, after having been under that responsibility for four years.

6. The groups of teachers at each of the three school levels are rewarded each year with autonomy in teaching, including choice of the number of students they will have responsibility for, with the reward based on the average level of achievement of children for whom they have been responsible for graduating over the past two years. This level of achievement determines the rank of the school for admissions purposes.

7. A child and her/his parents are rewarded for value added at a given level, with free tuition for postsecondary education, or for postsecondary vocational-technical training. The amount of free tuition depends on the amount of value added.

8. A child's level of performance at the end of a four-year stage of schooling determines the schools at the next stage to which he or she can apply. The school (i.e., the group of teachers) determines the number of students they will accept (a decision which will affect their potential salary bonus, which depends upon total--not average--value added). Teachers cannot choose which students they will have. Students' priority in admission, when a school is oversubscribed, is determined by their level of achievement on the examination just taken. The group of teachers which constitutes a high school must contract with specialist teachers for the specialized area of each student in their care. Specialist teachers will teach or coach students from more than one school.

9. The cohort of students at a given age level in a school is rewarded each year *as a group* for the total value added for the group for that year. The reward, given each year on the basis of that year's value added, consists of a certificate valuable for purchasing school

resources (for example, computers, audio-visual or other technology aids) to be used by that cohort during its tenure in the school, and then left with the school when the cohort graduates. The decision about how to spend the certificate is made jointly by students, parents, and teachers.

10. The group of teachers responsible for a given level of students (four years) should be between 4 and 16. This is the group of teachers who are rewarded together (see 5 and 6) for joint performance. There is no principal. Decisions are made collectively by the group of teachers who constitute the school. There may be more than one school in a building. Schools in the same building may use community resources (health, welfare, and other agencies) housed in the same building.

11. The academic subject examinations should involve demonstration of achievement in each area tested. This may require a portion of the test to be in performance, rather than only paper-and-pencil. Although more expensive, this implies taking each student seriously, and creates an incentive toward more extensive preparation. It is already part of the examination at the end of secondary school in some countries.

12. If the child's level of performance was below that which would permit admission in any school at the next level (which would occur only if there were too few places for the number of students, an event that would probably not occur), then the child would be required to repeat a year in the current school. However, if a child's test score did not make possible admission to a school acceptable to the child and her parents, the child could choose to repeat a year, with the aim of improving performance.

13. Any set of teachers, each of whom satisfied state qualification requirements, could set up a school, so long as they would have a certain minimum number of students. Their initial position in the rank of schools is at the bottom.

14. The school would be required to take responsibility for the student during a certain period of each weekday, and the student is required to attend the school. The school may offer to some or all students the option of spending a greater portion of each day at school, and the student and parent may choose whether to accept

such offers. [This provision differs little from the existing extracurricular activities (sports, drama, etc.) that are carried out after school, except that it also includes the possibility of curricular activities.]

Design 2. This design is like that of Design 1, except for the provisions noted below. The design differs from Design 1 principally in the possibility for some children in the middle and high schools to spend part of their school time as assistant teachers in lower schools.

1. At the middle school and the high school, students with the highest value added in a given year will have the choice of spending half of their school time in the next year as an assistant teacher in elementary school (for middle school students) and elementary or middle school (for high school students). The student is qualified to be an assistant teacher in any school in which the average entry test score is below that student's entry test score. The choice is made anew for each year in middle school and in high school. Students' options are in the order of value added, and may be revoked during the year of their tenure by their master teacher.

2. The student who chooses to spend half of her/his time as an assistant teacher will receive tuition expenses for half a year of postsecondary education or vocational training; or if this is a fee-paying school, will pay only half tuition for that year. In addition, assistant teachers participate in the bonuses received by the school they are teaching in, but at a reduced level compared to the regular teachers' bonuses.

Design 3. This design is based on an incentive structure which depends on interscholastic competition. Here, rather than achievement level being judged by performance on a standardized test, it is judged by success in interscholastic competition. Except for the provisions noted below, this design is like Design 1.

1. External tests are replaced by frequent interscholastic competitions involving both team and individual performances. Models for these already exist in some areas, such as interscholastic mathematics team competitions, debates, and statewide contests involving both academic subjects and the performing arts. The

competitions would be in the form of tournaments (round-robin or otherwise).

2. On a certain core of subjects, each student would participate; for other subjects and more advanced performance in the core subjects, students would select the areas in which they wanted to compete.

3. The tournament competitions described in Design 1 would lead to individual and team rankings. The individual ranking covers all students in the core subject areas, and only subsets of students in the non-core subject areas.

4. The "value added" or "gains" of a student in Design 1 are determined in Design 3 by the differences in rank (combined rank over all subjects contested) over the year or at the entrance to and exit from a given school. The "level" of performance of a student at the time of completion of a given school (elementary, middle, high) is determined in Design 3 by the student's rank at the time of exit from that school. With this modification, all of the Design 1 principles which depend on measurement of value added or level of performance apply to Design 3. (There may be a necessity to measure the actual levels of performance in terms of content rather than rank. This can be determined by measuring the content learned by a small sample of persons at different ranks.)

Current Developments Toward Output-Driven Schools

There are several current developments in American education which constitute movements toward output-driven schools. These developments are primarily toward one aspect of school design, that is, the use of externally designed and administered standards. It is important to note that unless the introduction of external standards is used not only for evaluation of level of performance, but also for evaluation of performance gain, it will not be widely accepted in American schools, because of the disadvantage it creates for non-high-performing students, their parents, and their teachers.

One development is Congressional legislation to establish national standards. Although it is too early to know the character of these standards, and how they will be used, the establishment of such standards is a departure from the past in American education. In some states, similar legislation has recently been passed. A much more minor development, but one in the same direction, is the publication of sample university entrance examinations from several countries in selected subject areas. The first of these, in biology, from English A-levels, the German Abitur, the French Baccalaureate, Japanese university entrance tests, and the U.S. Advanced Placement test, has been published. The American Federation of Teachers is responsible for this publication effort.

In several states, "charter schools" are being established with public funding. They are operated not by public education authorities, but often by groups of interested teachers. The continued funding of each charter school will depend upon student performance criteria established by the public education authorities. Attempts have also been made in several cities (Baltimore, Minneapolis, and Hartford) to place some of the schools in the district under the operation of a private contractor. The contractor is required to meet certain student performance standards in order for the contract to be renewed.

The charter school and the contracting out developments have an important element in common. When public education authorities operate schools, they have a conflict of interest. As representatives of the public, they have the consumer's interest, specifically an interest in holding the providers of education accountable for an education of high quality at reasonable cost. But, as operators of the schools, they have the interests of any supplier of a good or service: an interest in not being held accountable for the quality of the good or service. When public education authorities forego operation of the schools, through chartering schools or contracting out, they no longer have a conflict of interest. As representatives of the public, they are in a position to hold accountable the providers (charter schools, contractors). The public authorities then become the parties which can establish external standards.

One likely objection to output-driven school design is the possibility of a negative impact on minorities who have either a linguistic or other disadvantage. There are two responses to such an objection. First, schools have traditionally rewarded only level of achievement. An essential element of the output-driven design presented here is that students are rewarded both for level of achievement and for achievement gain, and teachers are rewarded primarily for their students' achievement gain. The rewards for achievement gain, properly calibrated, are just as attainable for students at a low level of achievement as for those at a high level. It is in this respect that the output-driven design presented here differs most strongly from existing school systems that use external achievement criteria (as, for example, most European systems do).

Second, such an objection is based on the assumption that stronger academic demands (which output-driven schools would bring about) lead to greater inequality and to higher dropout rates among disadvantaged students. This assumption is incorrect. For example, a recent study of course-taking in American schools reports,

> (T)he recent process of raising academic standards in high school by strengthening graduation requirements and reducing the number of electives that students may take has moved us closer to the goal of equal educational opportunity for larger numbers of students than ever before in our history. No group has responded more positively to these changes than African American students who have increased their proportion of academic course-taking more dramatically than whites. Equally striking is the fact that during the very time that high school standards were being raised, the dropout rate fell, particularly among black students (Mirel and Angus 1994, 41).

Current Development Away from Output-Driven Schools

There have always been strong leveling impulses in American education. One form that these levelling impulses have taken in recent years is opposition to standardized testing. Standardized tests, largely of the multiple-choice variety, have been the principal externally designed and externally administered tests of school achievement. These tests, used both internally by schools to track their students' performance and at the end of high school in college admission, have been widely criticized for both good and bad reasons. The good reason is that such tests are poorer measures of achievement than are other measures which make fewer compromises with the time of the test-taker and the test-scorer. The bad reason is that the tests, by giving each student a numerical score, introduce competition and invidious distinction.

Both these reasons have given rise to a movement in American education described as performance assessment. Performance assessment ordinarily involves some kind of performance, and may result in a "portfolio" of materials produced by the student. Performance assessment has much in common with the kinds of performances in music or drama auditions, or artists' portfolios, or athletic contests, all of which have long provided the basis for decisions on admission or scholarships to postsecondary institutions which provide further training for these skills. There is much to recommend these methods of assessment. There are, of course, practical problems in implementing these methods broadly, and in attempting to replace current grading systems or current standardized testing with these methods. It is these practical problems, principally the time required to obtain an assessment, which have prevented them from being more widely used at present. Were these practical problems to be overcome, the performances, demonstrations, and portfolios of performances could replace current standardized testing.

However, there are certain aspects of performance assessment which constitute a threat to high achievement in American schools. The threat they pose is not inherent in performance assessment, but lies in the ease with which performance assessment can be made compatible with reduced performance levels by those who would eliminate competition in schools. Some elements of performance assessment which make it easily shaped to fit these interests are:

1. Assessments in many disciplines are not objective but subjective, depending on judges' evaluations.

2. Most current prescriptions for performance assessment in schools do not make use of external evaluations, but depend on the teachers themselves. Thus, the principle of an output-driven organization is missing. In some forms of performance assessment, there is no comparative evaluation of students' performances at all; the merit is in the eye of the beholder. In this, current proposals for performance assessment are unlike their forebears, in which external judges determine the awarding of admission or scholarships on the basis of performance or portfolios.

3. The creation of a portfolio, while purportedly the work of the student, may well include significant contributions by the teacher, who has an incentive to make her or his students' performance appear impressive to parents. Such contributions by the teacher may be easier than developing the skill in the student.

4. The ambiguity of evaluations of performances can reduce or remove altogether the incentive of student, parent, and teacher toward improved performance.

The threat to output-driven schools is not inherent in performance assessment. There is much that can be taken from performance-oriented approaches that can greatly improve current standardized testing. However, it seems quite possible that the strongest drive toward performance assessment comes from the levelling impulse, i.e., from the aim of eliminating comparative evaluation in schools. The levelling impulse has already led American schools down an unfruitful path. Rather than eliminate or reduce standards, the fruitful direction is to redirect comparison of the student's performance with his or her own earlier performance. This provides a measure of the value added for that student by the school, and places all students on an equal footing.

There is a broader movement, with which performance assessment is associated, called "Outcome-Based Education" (OBE). Outcome-based education originally was a response to a demand, primarily from business, legislatures, and elsewhere outside the education establishment, to hold educational institutions accountable for their product through measurement of achievement via standardized tests. As Manno (1994) points out, however, implementation of the intent of legislatures or state boards of education was, in those states which had such mandates (36, according to the Education Commission of the States), carried out by those who were interested in expanding the goals of education in affective directions and blurring academic goals. Thus, the "outcomes" produced by these groups included such things as "All students understand and appreciate their worth as unique and capable individuals and exhibit self-esteem" (State of Virginia), and "Understand diversity and the interdependence of people" (State of Minnesota). Apart from the expansion toward affective outcomes, the outcomes were expressed in vague terms, as if designed so that no student could fail to meet the standards, and no school could be held accountable for students' poor performance.

None of the developments toward or away from output-driven schools treat the combination of elements that make up an output-driven design. Most focus on a single element, external standards, either moving toward externally designed and administered standards, to raise levels of performance, or away from such standards, to reduce competitiveness in schools and invidious distinction between those toward the top and those toward the bottom. If there are to be successful output-driven schools, in which achievement is high and children at all points in the distribution of achievement see their efforts rewarded, then all six of the analytical elements listed previously, as necessary, must be present. I have sketched three possible designs of schools and school systems which contain these six elements. These, of course, are only three among many. They differ sharply, however, as I suspect any effective output-driven design will do, from the organization of education found in America today.

3

A Comparison of 1980 and 1990 Sophomore Mathematics Achievement

Huayin Wang, Kathryn S. Schiller, and Stephen Plank

Issues in Estimating Changes in Student Achievement

Student academic performance in the U. S. has been the subject of ongoing debate and concern among policy makers, researchers, and the general public. In addition to the seemingly basic question of whether high school test scores have improved or declined during the past several decades, there are more complex questions such as what effect demographic shifts and recent school reforms have had on student achievement. Central to this debate are the issues of what students know and what they need to know. The lack of definitive evidence or convincing answers to these questions has contributed to public uncertainty about the effectiveness of American schools in helping students succeed academically.

The viewpoint that we need to dramatically improve academic achievement has been presented in reports such as *A Nation at Risk* (National Commission on Excellence in Education 1983). Ten years later, this same message was echoed in the document, *Raising Standards for American Education* (National Council on Education Standards and Testing 1992). After more than a decade of concerns about the effectiveness of schools to improve student achievement, the emergence of new state and federal legislation was hardly surprising, most notably the *Goals 2000, Educate America Act*, that was passed by Congress in 1994.

Much of the disappointment and frustration that has been expressed about American academic achievement stems from trend reports of Scholastic Aptitude Test (SAT) results and from international studies comparing the performance of American high school students with students in other industrialized nations (Ravitch 1995; Steinberg, Brown and Dornbusch 1996). Regarding the SAT, a standardized exam taken by high school students seeking to enter college, scores have fallen considerably since the mid-1960's. Even though there was a slight rebound during the early 1980's, SAT scores have not returned to their pre-1975 levels (Ravitch 1995). While SAT declines have often been attributed to demographic changes in the test-taking population, detailed analyses suggest that only a small part of the decline can be explained by these changes. (See summaries of these analyses in Ravitch 1995 and Steinberg, Brown and Dornbusch 1996.)

With regard to international comparisons, much of the evidence comes from the International Association for the Evaluation of Educational Achievement (IEA) (Husen 1967; Elley 1992) and the International Assessment of Educational Progress (IAEP) (Lapointe, Mead and Askew 1992a & 1992b). The general conclusion drawn by most researchers is that, while American students do well on tests of literacy compared to other countries' students, Americans do very poorly in all areas of mathematics and science. The U.S. international rankings in these areas have fallen over time and are especially low among older students (Linn and Baker 1995; Bronfenbrenner, McClelland, Wethington, Moen, and Ceci 1996).

Although many people give considerable credence to the data on SAT trends and international comparisons, others either question the appropriateness of using these data (Crouse and Trusheim 1988; Powell and Steelman 1984) or take issue with the pessimistic diagnosis of the state of American academic performance (Berliner and Biddle 1995). Those skeptical of drawing conclusions from SAT trends warn of the severe selection bias that occurs if the demographic profiles of students who self-select to take the SAT change markedly over a span of years. Those dubious of drawing conclusions from international comparisons note that there is considerable variation among participating countries regarding sample selection and data collection techniques (Linn and Baker 1995). In some countries with strong centralized school systems, curricular content is closely aligned with test score items. This is less for countries like the U.S. where what is covered in particular classrooms is subject to variations in both state requirements and local practices (Stevenson and Baker 1991). Until quite recently, international data sets also tended to lack a rich set of individual and family background variables that are factors strongly related to achievement.

Even among those who are willing to use SAT scores or international exam data to chart educational trends, one finds disagreement regarding explanations for the decline in SAT scores and the poor performance of American students in comparison with students in other countries. Researchers list many factors that may explain the apparent decline of American achievement, from the quality of instruction and the organization of curriculum, to the weakening of traditional family values, increased television viewing, and decreased time devoted to homework.

The assessment of schools and schooling is a very complicated issue in part because educational outcomes are a function of a great number of interrelated influences which must be measured and accounted for in analyses of student achievement. Not withstanding the difficulties of assessment, and considering that schools are responsible for many outcomes in addition to academic achievement, the tracing of achievement trends remains very important and strongly demanded.

Our perspective and objectives in this chapter are as follows: We recognize that little consensus can be reached as to whether there has been a decline in American students' academic achievement and, if so, how severe the decline has been. One way to adjudicate the lack of agreement would be to conduct analyses based on reliable measures of achievement that can be examined from a comparative perspective, either between countries or across time. We have already indicated some of the potential problems with cross-national comparisons. Drawing several conclusions from prior studies, we eventually determined that international studies do not serve our purposes primarily because the distribution of the demographic characteristics of examination takers varies substantively between countries. Another approach is the comparison of American students' achievement over time, such as the trend reports for SAT scores and the National Assessment of Educational Progress (NAEP). While these sources are useful, they leave certain questions unanswered. For example, analyses of SAT trends continue to be plagued by the potential for selection bias. NAEP does not include many social and economic background variables at the student and school levels. Without the ability to control on these background variables, analyses based on NAEP are limited in their usefulness.

We then turned to analyses of the High School and Beyond (HS&B) and the National Education Longitudinal Study of 1988-1994 (NELS:88-94) data sets. These two longitudinal studies contain representative samples of American sophomores in 1980 and 1990, and thus provide a rare opportunity for comparative studies of achievement levels across time. The data are of high quality, include many social and economic background measures, and, most importantly, have mathematics achievement test scores that are comparable due to the presence of a sufficient number of common items on the two studies' test batteries.

International Mathematics and Science Study

Several international studies have been conducted by the IEA during the past three decades. The First International Mathematics Study in 1964 involved twelve countries with 13-year-olds as the target population. The Second International Mathematics Study, in the early 1980's, involved 13-

year-olds from eighteen countries, and students in the last year of secondary education in thirteen countries. Two corresponding science studies were also conducted from 1966 to 1973 and from 1983 to 1986. The research reports of all of these studies suggested a consistent finding: American students lagged behind others, particularly in mathematics.

These IEA studies might have received less attention, or at least might have been less controversial, if the findings about the international test performance standings of American students had been different. If, for example, the studies had found that American students scored highest among the students in industrialized countries, many issues such as the limitations of the data and the pitfalls of the sampling design might have been easily forgiven or never even raised by American policy makers and researchers. A high standing for American students, however, was not what the studies found.

Subsequently, these findings as well as issues of sampling bias, test bias, and the quality of the studies have been the subjects of numerous debates and controversies. Various explanations for the differences in achievement among countries have also been explored. A re-evaluation of the data and results by the U.S. Department of Education concluded that the credibility of the results holds. The re-evaluation concluded that despite methodological concerns, the findings of the international surveys were consistent, powerful, and not to be discounted. "The international surveys do help determine 'where we stand' in mathematics and science achievement--that is, the performance of American students as compared with students from other countries" (Medrich and Griffith 1992). Unfortunately, compared to those students from other countries, American students did not perform well.

Because of the complex nature of international comparisons, any explanations given for the poor performance of American students should be treated as tentative. Also, we should remember that most of these debates are about the Second International Mathematics Study, which occurred over a decade ago. We are aware that the Third International Mathematics and Science Study is currently underway and we suspect that the data obtained from this initiative will help resolve some of these issues. But perhaps more important to our interest is the question of how different the test scores of American students from the 1980's are to the 1990's? Has achievement improved, or has there been a continuous decline in achievement over the past twenty years? It is to these types of domestic comparisons which we now turn.

Achievement Over Time

Trends for SAT scores have contributed, perhaps more than anything else, to the general perception of declining achievement in the U.S. The SAT is a standardized, multiple-choice test with verbal and mathematical sections with scores ranging from 200 to 800. As Ravitch (1995) reports:

> Beginning in 1964 average SAT scores dropped steadily for about fifteen years. Verbal scores fell from a high of 478 in 1963 down to the 420s by the late 1970s and hovered there; they stood at 423 in 1994. Mathematics scores dropped from a high of 502 in 1963 to a low of 466 in 1980, and then moved up to 479 by 1994, about where they had been in 1974 (p.64).

Many people have claimed that the SAT drop between the 1960's and 1980 was due to changes in the test-taking population; to an increasing proportion of high school students taking the exam, and, specifically, to an increasing proportion of minority and low-income students taking the exam. Several analyses refute this explanation, however. As Ravitch points out, the decline in SAT scores continued even during years in which the number of students taking the test did not increase appreciably. Further, as Steinberg, Brown, and Dornbusch (1996) report, the decline in performance among white students was identical to the overall drop in scores, indicating that this larger pattern of decline resulted neither from "the democratization of the test nor ... the expansion of educational opportunities to ethnic minorities" (p. 31). In summary, SAT trends suggest a broad pattern of decline between the late 1960's and the early 1980's, followed by a moderate increase beginning in the early 1980's. Analyses of NAEP showed a similar pattern for the same age group. From 1973 to 1982 there was a pattern of declines in performance, followed by a recovery during the late 1980's.

Moreover, both SAT and NAEP mathematics trends also showed that from the late 1970's to the late 1980's, minority students actually had greater achievement gains than white students did. A recent report using data from NELS:88-94 and HS&B reveals similar findings (Rasinski, Ingels, Rock, Pollack and Wu 1993). This report states that (1) between 1980 and 1990 sophomores increased their skills significantly in mathematics achievement, and (2) African American and Hispanic students made proportionately greater gains than their white and Asian American counterparts.

Analyses of the SAT and NAEP are informative for obtaining general trends in achievement over time. However, at a more specific level they are limited because of the inability to control for background characteristics of test takers. For example, SAT scores exist, of course, for only those students who take the exam. Thus, SAT trends tell us nothing about the more than fifty percent of high school students who never take the exam (Ravitch 1995). To more adequately address questions of how American student achievement has changed over time, we need analyses based upon nationally representative samples of students at multiple time points and which include measures of individual, family, and school background characteristics. Given these considerations, we now turn to analyses of the HS&B and NELS:88-94 data.

Mathematics Achievement: High School Sophomores in 1980 and 1990

HS&B and NELS:88-94 offer the rare opportunity to compare achievement trends at time points ten years apart, while controlling on important background measures. The most important feature of these two data sets is that their mathematics test batteries share enough common items that equating procedures can put test scores of students from both data sets on the same scale. The equating process, based on Item Response Theory (IRT), involves using an individual's pattern of answers to estimate an "ability" score (Rock, Pollack and Quinn 1995). This measure is then transformed into the "IRT-Estimated Number Right" score. After this equating process, HS&B and NELS:88-94 IRT scores can be directly compared. The IRT scores used in this chapter were provided by the Educational Testing Service (ETS).

Figure 3.1 shows a comparison of the distributions of the HS&B and NELS:88-94 sophomores in terms of their mathematics test scores. The curves represent the test score distributions of HS&B and NELS:88-94, respectively, with the two vertical lines in the middle representing the positions of the mean test scores for the corresponding samples. We can see that the 1990 sophomores on average achieved higher test scores than the 1980 sophomore cohort. (Note that the solid vertical line, which represents the NELS:88-94 mean, is to the right of the dotted vertical line, which represents the HS&B mean.) The mean test score increased by about 3 points (approximately 0.26 standard deviations within the pooled 1980/1990 sophomore distribution) over the ten years.

Figure 3.2 provides another look at the same data in which test scores are plotted against the percentile ranking (in terms of test scores) within each cohort. In other words, this figure shows what ranking within his or

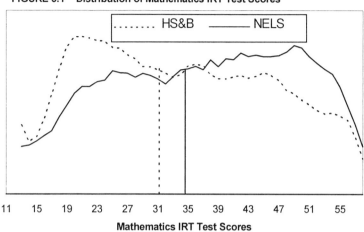

FIGURE 3.1   Distribution of Mathematics IRT Test Scores

Mathematics IRT Test Scores

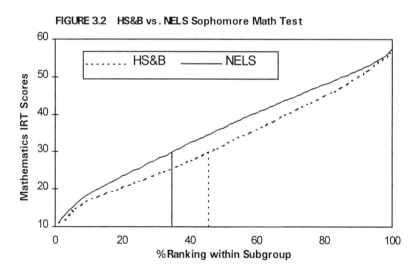

FIGURE 3.2   HS&B vs. NELS Sophomore Math Test

her cohort a student with a given test score would have. The solid line
which represents NELS:88-94 sophomores' test profile is above the dotted
line which represents the HS&B sophomores. This aspect of the graph
reflects the fact that a sophomore in 1990 had to achieve a higher score to
hold the same ranking as a sophomore in 1980.

Another way to summarize Figure 3.2 is to say that a given test score would have been associated with a lower percentile ranking in 1990 than it would have been associated with in 1980. To offer a specific example, the dotted vertical line in Figure 3.2 shows that a student with a score of 30 would have been ranked in the 46th percentile in the HS&B cohort while the solid vertical line shows that the same score of 30 would have been associated with only the 35th percentile in the NELS:88-94 cohort. We can also see that the difference in test scores between the median NELS:88-94 and HS&B sophomores (those corresponding to the 50th percentile) is about 5 points. The conclusions to be drawn from Figures 3.1 and 3.2 are consistent with other studies, such as the SAT and NAEP analyses, which show achievement gains during the 1980's.

Subgroup Comparisons

While sophomores are, overall, performing better on tests in 1990 compared to 1980, we do not know whether these increases are found among all students or whether changes in test scores vary by students' background or school characteristics. To identify which subgroups, as defined by various demographic characteristics, gained most between 1980 and 1990, we compare their achievement means and gains at these two time points. For example, change in mean test scores between 1980 and 1990 for public school enrollees is compared to that for Catholic school enrollees. Similarly, we can compare the change in mean test scores for African American students with the change for white students. These comparisons are important because they indicate how the increases in academic achievement are related to changes in students' backgrounds or school experiences.

While many comparisons are interesting, we selected eight variables that identify important subgroups which consistently vary in their academic performance. The first set of variables relates to students' social backgrounds. These include *socioeconomic status* (with subgroups defined by quartiles), *gender* (with male and female as subgroups), *race/ethnicity* (with Asian American, Hispanic, African American, and white as subgroups), *parental level of education* (with "less than high school graduation," "high school graduation," "more than high school but less than college graduation," and "college graduation or more" as subgroups).[1] Students' educational goals and efforts to realize them may also have changed from 1980 to 1990, making it important to compare the achievement of students by their *educational expectation* (with subgroups again defined as they are for parents' education) and *high school program* (with general, academic, and vocational as subgroups). Finally, changes in achievement may vary by the types of schools in which students enroll, particularly between *school sectors* (with public, Catholic, and other private as subgroups) and *urbanicity of the school* (with urban, suburban, and rural as subgroups). These comparisons will show whether the increases in test scores between 1980 and 1990 were universal or isolated to particular groups.

Tables 3.1a and 3.1b show the comparison of the mean mathematics test scores for each indicated subgroup in 1980 and 1990. We have also calculated the difference in the mean test scores (the NELS:88-94 mean test score minus the HS&B mean test score). A t-statistic for the estimated difference is also provided (see Appendix 3.1 for details of calculation).

Results in Table 3.1a show that nearly all subgroups show positive gains between 1980 and 1990. Using a t-statistic of 2.00 as the indicator of statistical significance, we find that all subgroups showed positive gains except two race/ethnic groups: Asian Americans and Native Americans. Similarly in Table 3.1b, significant changes are found for all but two subgroups, those students who were not sure they would graduate from or pursue their education past high school.

However, with sample sizes as large as those for HS&B and NELS:88-94, even very small differences can be statistically significant. For this reason, it is also useful to consider the substantive significance of cohort differences. Based on the concept of "effect size" (Glass and Hopkins, 1984) we propose considering differences of two or more IRT points as representing a difference of substantive significance. Using this criterion, some of the differences considered significant using the previous measure do not have substantive meaning. For example, the initially striking decline in scores for students who plan to attend but not complete college is not substantively meaningful because the difference is very small. Other differences which are not substantively significant are those for subgroups whose parents did not complete college (Table 3.1a), and students in vocational programs and suburban schools (Table 3.1b).

Results for the subgroups characterized by level of educational expectation are especially interesting. Consider the fact that when we compare students from the two cohorts at any given level of educational expectation there are no substantively significant differences in achievement. However, when we compare the two cohorts as a whole, significant gains are seen between 1980 and 1990. How is it possible that for the population as a whole there are significant gains, while there is practically no gain for any of the subgroups characterized by educational expectation? The answer lies in the fact that, on average, students in 1990 had considerably higher educational expectations than did students in 1980. If we look at the weighted percentages in Table 3.1b, we can see, for example, that about 60 percent of the NELS:88-94 sophomores expected

TABLE 3.1a Mathematics Test Scores Comparisons by Students'
Social Backgrounds

	HS&B		NELS:88		Difference in Scores	T-value
	Wt.Pct	Scores	Wt.Pct	Scores		
All Students	100.00	32.81	100.00	35.97	3.16	14.36
SES						
Low	24.5%	26.93	22.1%	29.17	2.24	6.45
M-Low	25.4%	31.65	24.9%	34.10	2.44	6.58
M-High	24.8%	34.58	26.1%	37.15	2.58	6.90
High	25.3%	39.53	26.9%	42.90	3.37	10.07
Race/Ethnicity						
Asian	1.1%	38.82	3.7%	40.26	1.44	1.14
Hispanic	12.9%	25.96	9.9%	30.75	4.79	9.76
Black	12.0%	24.51	12.8%	28.74	4.23	8.02
White	72.8%	35.41	72.2%	37.96	2.55	11.21
Native	1.1%	27.24	1.4%	27.02	-0.22	-0.14
Gender						
Male	49.8%	33.02	50.3%	36.06	3.03	9.49
Female	50.2%	32.60	49.7%	35.89	3.29	10.95
Parent Education						
< HS	13.7%	26.76	8.7%	27.93	1.18	2.02
HS	34.3%	31.16	21.2%	32.25	1.08	2.45
>HS	28.6%	34.59	41.4%	35.60	1.01	2.70
College	23.4%	39.89	28.6%	42.61	2.72	6.95

to have four or more years of college education. This contrasts with about
40 percent of the HS&B sophomores. It is the increase in the overall level
of educational expectations rather than an increase in test scores at a given
level of educational expectations that accounts for the overall gain in mean
test scores.

The changes in the weighted percentages in Tables 3.1a and 3.1b reflect
compositional changes in the American sophomore population during this
ten-year span, while the changes in test scores reflect gains in achievement
within each of the corresponding subgroups. For each variable used to
classify students into subgroups (i.e., SES, race/ethnicity, gender, etc.), we
can decompose the changes in mean test scores between the HS&B and
NELS:88 full samples into those differences due to compositional changes

TABLE 3.1b Mathematics Test Scores Comparisons by School Related Factors

	HS&B		NELS:88		Difference in Scores	T-value
	Wt.Pct	Scores	Wt.Pct	Scores		
Student Characteristics						
Educational Expectation						
< HS	2.0%	22.35	0.6%	23.10	0.75	0.37
HS	24.8%	26.13	9.6%	26.77	0.64	1.19
>HS	33.1%	31.48	30.9%	30.70	-0.78	-2.14
College	40.1%	39.30	58.8%	40.50	1.20	4.27
High School Program						
General	46.6%	30.97	42.2%	35.20	4.24	13.75
Academic	32.8%	39.79	33.9%	42.35	2.56	8.31
Vocational	20.6%	26.65	9.9%	28.28	1.63	2.89
Other/DK			13.9%	29.26		
School Characteristics						
Urbanicity						
Urban	20.0%	30.41	27.6%	36.03	5.63	13.16
Suburban	47.4%	34.35	56.7%	36.28	1.93	6.66
Rural	32.6%	32.05	15.7%	35.25	3.19	7.32
School Sector						
Public	90.5%	32.22	90.5%	35.45	3.23	14.62
Catholic	6.2%	38.11	5.8%	40.72	2.62	4.06
Other Private	3.3%	38.96	3.7%	42.20	3.24	2.53

and those due to gains in test scores within subgroups. In the case of gender, for example, there is almost no difference in the proportion of males and females in HS&B and NELS:88-94. The main component in the test score increase is, therefore, the achievement gains for each subgroup. In the case of educational expectations, the main component is the compositional shift toward higher educational expectations. When subgroups are defined by parental education, we see both components (compositional change and achievement gains within subgroups) being somewhat influential.

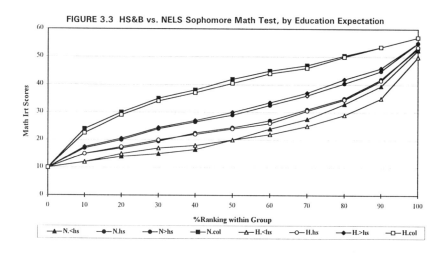

FIGURE 3.3 HS&B vs. NELS Sophomore Math Test, by Education Expectation

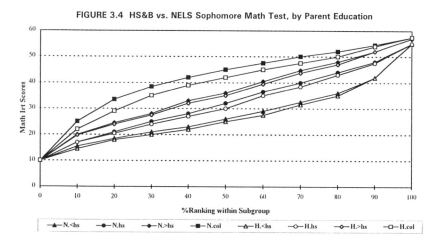

FIGURE 3.4 HS&B vs. NELS Sophomore Math Test, by Parent Education

The compositional changes associated with educational expectations and parental education are really quite striking. To explore the implications of these shifts further, Figures 3.3 and 3.4 provide more detail about achievement distributions for subgroups defined by educational expectation and parental education. As shown in Figure 3.3, students with the same level of educational expectation in HS&B and NELS:88-94 scored on approximately the same curve. Figure 3.4 shows a similar plot with subgroups defined by parental education. We can see that for students with the same level of parental education in HS&B and NELS:88, the curves are very similar to one another except for the subgroup defined by parental education of college or more. The figure reveals the same finding seen earlier in Table 3.1a. If we compare subgroups of students with the same level of parental education in HS&B and NELS:88-94, we find practically no change in test scores, except for students whose parents have four or more years of college.

Taken together, Table 3.1a and Figures 3.1 and 3.2 indicate a discomforting finding. Namely, that despite advances in educational technology, improvements in teaching techniques, waves of school reform, and increases in funding, students from families with lower parental educational backgrounds did not reap major benefits during the 1980's. This fact indicates how important parental education is as a social and economic background variable and, thus, the need to control it when assessing the amount of progress we have made in providing high quality schooling. When the relative gains of students in different types of schools and programs are assessed, any differences in their student compositions in terms of family background should be considered. In the following section, we will look in more detail at the comparison of student achievement between subgroups with their parental education being controlled.

Achievement Gains Controlling for Parental Education

In Tables 3.2a and 3.2b, we divided selected subgroups into four further subclassifications according to the level of parental education. These comparisons will show whether achievement gains are uniform across the various subgroups, and thus independent of the level of parental education. This also allows us to see how much of the overall achievement gain between 1980 and 1990 is due to the increase in the level of parental education and the increase when the level of parental education is controlled. The subgroups for these more detailed comparisons were selected because they showed substantive gains between 1980 and 1990 and are related to educational stratification. Table 3.2a shows the differences for three racial/ethnic groups and high school programs, and Table 3.2b for different types of schools.

Looking at racial and ethnic categories in Table 3.2a, the patterns of achievement gains varies between subgroups. For white students, the greatest gains in achievement occurred for those whose parents had at least four years of college, but there were no significant gains for those whose parents have less than a college degree. The patterns for both Hispanic and

TABLE 3.2a Mathematics Test Scores Comparison for Parent Education Groups by Students' Social Backgrounds

		HS&B		NELS:88		Difference	
		Wt. Pct	Scores	Wt.Pct	Scores	in Scores	T-value
Race/Ethnicity							
Hispanic							
	< HS	27.9%	23.72	31.9%	27.87	4.15	5.38
	HS	35.0%	26.04	19.2%	30.12	4.08	3.78
	> HS	23.2%	27.24	35.8%	32.58	5.35	5.83
	Coll.	13.8%	32.97	13.1%	36.81	3.84	2.59
Black							
	< HS	22.4%	23.02	13.5%	25.04	2.02	1.73
	HS	35.2%	24.66	23.9%	26.66	2.01	1.94
	> HS	28.5%	26.05	47.9%	29.32	3.27	3.69
	Coll.	13.9%	28.38	14.7%	34.93	6.56	4.24
White							
	< HS	10.1%	29.22	4.8%	28.98	-0.24	-0.28
	HS	34.3%	33.05	21.4%	33.67	0.61	1.34
	> HS	29.5%	36.69	41.4%	37.19	0.51	1.35
	Coll.	26.2%	41.32	32.4%	43.47	2.15	5.89
High School Program							
General							
	< HS	15.3%	26.46	7.7%	28.15	1.69	1.96
	HS	37.5%	29.88	23.0%	31.99	2.11	3.47
	> HS	28.2%	32.98	41.7%	34.89	1.90	3.74
	Coll.	18.9%	37.10	27.7%	41.02	3.91	6.50
Academic							
	< HS	7.5%	33.42	4.4%	35.58	2.16	1.56
	HS	25.4%	37.94	16.2%	38.69	0.75	0.99
	> HS	30.3%	39.69	39.4%	41.39	1.69	3.19
	Coll.	36.9%	43.59	40.1%	45.87	2.28	5.31
Vocational							
	< HS	19.8%	23.32	17.6%	25.70	2.38	2.06
	HS	42.4%	27.16	29.0%	26.16	-1.00	-1.03
	> HS	26.6%	28.96	43.4%	29.58	0.62	0.63
	Coll.	11.2%	30.54	10.0%	33.14	2.60	1.33

TABLE 3.2b Mathematics Test Scores Comparison for Parent
Education Groups by School Characteristics

		HS&B		NELS:88		Difference	
		Wt. Pet	Scores	Wt.Pct	Scores	in Scores	T-value
Urbanicity							
Urban							
	< HS	16.9%	25.72	10.1%	28.00	2.27	2.22
	HS	33.5%	29.48	17.6%	30.65	1.17	1.25
	> HS	29.6%	32.54	41.9%	35.98	3.44	4.40
	Coll.	20.0%	38.31	30.4%	42.77	4.47	5.49
Suburban							
	< HS	9.9%	28.21	7.8%	28.07	-0.15	-0.17
	HS	31.9%	32.00	21.1%	32.66	0.67	1.16
	> HS	29.5%	35.21	41.0%	35.57	0.37	0.75
	Coll.	28.7%	40.58	30.2%	42.81	2.24	4.53
Rural							
	< HS	17.3%	26.10	10.1%	27.58	1.48	1.35
	HS	38.5%	30.98	27.6%	33.18	2.20	2.81
	> HS	26.7%	34.87	41.6%	36.00	1.13	1.57
	Coll.	17.7%	39.29	20.7%	40.89	1.60	1.68
School Sector							
Public							
	< HS	14.6%	26.49	9.5%	27.87	1.38	2.51
	HS	35.4%	30.78	22.2%	32.04	1.26	2.96
	> HS	28.8%	34.27	42.6%	35.42	1.15	3.11
	Coll.	21.2%	39.54	25.7%	42.26	2.72	6.21
Catholic							
	< HS	4.9%	35.26	2.3%	32.32	-2.94	-0.96
	HS	28.5%	37.14	13.2%	36.84	-0.29	-0.19
	> HS	27.9%	38.43	35.2%	39.33	0.91	0.77
	Coll.	38.6%	40.10	49.3%	43.30	3.20	3.37

African American students show some increases in achievement for most
parental education levels. For both groups, parental education levels
increased substantially. In HS&B, 28.5 percent of African American
students and 23.2 percent of Hispanic students had parents with more than

a high school education but less than four years of college, compared to 47.9 and 35.8 percent respectively in NELS:88-94. However, these increases do not account for all of the gains in achievement for these two groups.

For Hispanic students, there is a fairly uniform and substantial test score gain, independent of their parents educational backgrounds. For African American students whose parents have no more than a high school education, achievement gains are fairly small (about 2 IRT points). However, there are substantial gains for those whose parents have more than a high school education, particularly those with college graduation or more.

Regarding high school curricular track placement also shown in Table 3.2a, those general track students whose parents had less than a college degree had small gains, while those whose parents had at least graduated from college had substantial gains. In somewhat similar fashion, academic track students whose parents had no more than a high school education showed no significant gains, while those whose parents attained more than a high school degree had small gains. The story is quite different for students in the vocational program. For these students, only those whose parents had less than a high school education showed significant (albeit small) gains. This comparison should be taken with caution, however, because the HS&B and NELS:88-94 questions about enrollment differed substantially.

With respect to school urbanicity in Table 3.2b, the gains among students whose parents did not go beyond high school education are either small or not significant. For urban students, only those with fairly high parental education (more than high school) showed substantial gains. A somewhat similar pattern exists with respect to school sector. In both public and Catholic schools, students whose parents earned less than a four-year college degree had no significant achievement gains. In contrast, however, those whose parents attained college graduation or more showed substantial positive gains between 1980 and 1990.

We can summarize our findings as follows: Test score comparisons between HS&B and NELS:88-94 show quite different patterns for sophomore groups with different parental education levels. Specifically, those whose parents had less than four years of college showed no substantively significant gains. In contrast, those whose parents had a college degree or more showed substantial gains. In all but the Hispanic and rural subgroups, students whose parents had a college degree or more showed the highest gains in achievement scores. This pattern remains, regardless of school type and program (except for the vocational program where the results are not conclusive). The pattern also holds true for African American and white students. The results suggest that students with less educated parents are severely disadvantaged and seem to have become increasingly disadvantaged between 1980 and 1990. Their disadvantage comes into even sharper relief when one considers that the population as a whole is becoming increasingly educated.

Conclusions

This chapter serves as an empirical starting point for the book's subsequent chapters. People are genuinely concerned about academic achievement because they perceive that it has very important implications for the quality of the nation's future workforce and the general health of American society. Based on various cross-national comparisons, and on internal comparisons between different socioeconomic groups, there is much concern that our schools are not producing the achievement they should or could produce.

And yet, the evidence from this chapter cautions us not to be too alarmist in our opinions about the state of American education. In the important area of mathematics, sophomores in 1990 were achieving at higher levels, on average, than those in 1980. We do not see in our comparisons evidence of a great decline in American achievement in recent years. Rather, we see genuine improvement.

In another sense, however, we need to ask ourselves whether we should be satisfied. When one thinks about the types of skills and knowledge America will need in the twenty-first century, it is clear that we must set our standards very high in what we expect from our schools. More than likely, it is simply not sufficient in today's world to claim that achievement has not declined, or that it has improved very slightly.

The current state of education is especially troubling when one sees that the achievement gains since 1980 have not accrued among all segments of the population equally. The greatest part of the achievement gains seems to have been driven by a compositional shift toward more highly educated parents and accompanying achievement gains for the children of highly educated parents. For students who have not been a part of this increase in the duration of education, and for many of those who have traditionally been viewed as being at-risk, low achievement continues. We are left to conclude that some segments of the population have not shared in recent gains and that we need to expect great things from our schools. With these concerns in mind, we now turn to analyses that reveal some of our best hopes for designing schools that are both excellent and equitable.

Notes

1. Details of the construction of these variables are given in Appendix 3.1.

Appendix 3.1: Technical Notes

The following technical notes are intended to provide some detailed information about the data and procedures used in this chapter. This allows our work to be replicated by others if desired.

Samples Used

This chapter uses data from two longitudinal studies, HS&B and NELS:88-94. HS&B began in 1980 with the collection of base year data from approximately 30,000 high school sophomores and 30,000 seniors. Within the HS&B sophomore cohort, that which we have used in this chapter, cognitive test data are available for 24,938 cases. In NELS:88-94, the corresponding sophomore data are the First Follow-Up data, collected in 1990. This wave of data comprises 20,706 cases, including enrolled sophomores (n=18,221), dropouts, and non-respondents.

There are several issues involved in selecting the appropriate groups from each cohort for the purposes of our comparisons. First, NELS:88-94 started with eighth graders, whereas HS&B started when the students were sophomores. Thus, the subgroup of students who dropped out of school between eighth and tenth grades in the NELS:88-94 sample has no corresponding population in the HS&B sample. For this reason, we have excluded the NELS:88-94 dropouts from our analyses. Further, we also have limited our subjects to those who have valid mathematics test scores because the central focus of this chapter is on the comparison of mathematics test performance. Based on the above selection criteria, we have 24,685 HS&B sophomores and 17,281 NELS:88-94 sophomores. Given those unweighted sample sizes, all estimations in this chapter are weighted. We use the base year test weight (BYTESTWT) for HS&B and the first follow-up questionnaire weight (F1QWT) for NELS:88-94.

Precision and Significance Testing

As stated above, the samples we use in the analyses are based on the sub-sample who have valid mathematics test scores. The appropriate weight variables are used to get valid estimates which generalize to the national population of sophomores. In order to make proper inferences and interpretation, we have calculated t-statistics for each comparison of mean test scores we reported. In calculating these statistics, the following formula is used:

$$t = (M_1 - M_2) / \text{sqrt}(d_1 \times se_1^2 + d_2 \times se_2^2)$$

where M_1 and M_2 are the estimates being compared, d_1 and d_2 are the corresponding design effects, and se_1 and se_2 are the corresponding standard errors. The use of these design-corrected standard errors is meant to correct the deviation of the actual sampling methods from simple random sampling. Because both HS&B and NELS:88-94 used multistage, clustered probability sample designs, the resulting statistics are less variable than they would have been from a simple random sample of the same size. The design effects for each subgroup we used here are taken from

Table 7.2 of the *HS&B Sample Design Report* (Frankel, Kohnke, Buonanno, and Tourangeau 1981) for HS&B sophomores, and Table 3.6-3 of the *NELS:88 First Follow-Up User's Manual* (Ingels, Scott, Lindmark, Frankel and Myers 1992) for NELS:88. For subgroups for which there are no design effects given in those published tables, we have used the average design effect instead.

As we stated earlier, because the HS&B sophomore mathematics test and the NELS:88-94 first Follow-Up mathematics test have sixteen items in common, we are able to put them on the same scale. The detailed test equating procedure was carried out by estimating the response parameters for the common items, based on item response theory (IRT), using the NELS:88-94 sample and then putting the remaining non-overlapping HS&B items on that scale. The ability to execute this equating procedure is a special advantage of the data that allows us to compare the simple difference in test performance across a ten-year span.

Variables Used

Although both HS&B and NELS:88-94 have very rich items, there are few items that are directly comparable. Fortunately, we do have some common items which make this chapter's analyses possible. The following is a description of the variables and codings we used:

1. Gender, SES, and Race/Ethnicity:

The gender variable comes from variable BB083 in the HS&B data and F1SEX in the NELS:88-94 data. For SES, we used the composite variables BYSESQ for HS&B, and F1SESQ for NELS:88-94. The composite variable RACE is used for HS&B, and F1RACE is used for NELS:88-94. Some cautions are necessary regarding the SES and RACE variables, because they were implemented and/or constructed in slightly different ways in HS&B and NELS:88-94. For example, the SES variable in HS&B was constructed using student data, whereas in ELS:88-94 it was constructed primarily from parent data. The format of the RACE item in the two studies' student questionnaires is also different; for example, there was no category for Hispanic in HS&B, as there was in NELS:88-94. For detailed information, the reader should consult the relevant user's manuals.

2. Parental Education and Student's Educational Expectation:

Parental education variables are constructed in the same way for HS&B and NELS:88-94. In NELS:88-94, F1PARED characterizes the highest level of education attained by either of the student's parents. It is constructed using the parent questionnaire data (BYP30 and BYP31). Student data (BYS34A and BYS34B) were used whenever parent data were not available. For freshened students in the NELS:88-94 first Follow-Up, the New Student Supplement questions F1N20A and F1N20B were used. The same procedure was applied in constructing the corresponding HS&B variable, for which parent data (PBB38 and PBB50) and student data (BB039 and BB042) were used. However, caution should be used here because there are disproportionately lower rates of available parent data in HS&B than in NELS:88-94. Note also that we have collapsed responses into four categories: 1) "finished less than high school," 2) "high school graduation but no more," 3) "some technical school or college but no college degree," and 4) "college degree or more."

Educational expectation variables are taken from BB065 and F1S49. These were recoded into four categories, matching those used for parental education.

3. *School Type and Urbanicity:*

The HS&B variable SCHTYPE and the NELS:88-94 variable G10CTRL1 were used and recoded to indicate school type. They were recoded into three categories: "public," "Catholic," and "other private." The HS&B variable SCHURB and the NELS:88-94 variable G10URBAN were used to indicate urbanicity. The original codings of these variables have been retained.

4. *High School Program:*

The HS&B variable BB002 and the NELS:88-94 composite variable F1HSPROG were used and recoded to indicate high school program. In the new coding scheme, there are three categories for HS&B: "general," "academic," and "vocational." The original codings "3" to "9" for BB002 are recoded as "vocational." In addition to these three categories, we retain one other for NELS:88-94 representing "other program / do not know." Our reasons for introducing this inconsistency between the HS&B and NELS:88-94 codings are that it is simply problematic to omit cases falling into the fourth category because there are many such cases, while it is also problematic to collapse "other program / do not know" into any of the other three categories because the appropriate collapsing probably varies case-by-case and we have little information to guide such a decision.

4

Academic Press, Sense of Community, and Student Achievement

Roger Shouse

Much of our discussion about "output-drivenness" has concerned various particular organizational arrangements of schools. The concept can also be used, however, to characterize a school's normative agenda. That is, we can describe as output-driven those schools in which daily activities, practices, experiences, and understandings complement and reinforce the importance of academic achievement. While nearly every principal will claim student achievement to be an important goal, it seems reasonable to expect variation in the degree to which their school organizational cultures are actually driven by academically oriented beliefs, values, and norms. Some school cultures, for example, may be oriented more toward other kinds of outcomes, such as student self-esteem, sense of belonging, or the establishment of positive and caring social relationships.

Of course, most Americans probably expect their schools to be academically challenging as well as socially supportive, and recent waves of school reform represent a response to such public perception. And yet, school reformers and policy makers often overlook the friction that can occur between these two types of educational goals. A longstanding body of research indicates, in fact, that schools sometimes keep their students cooperative, satisfied, and socially attached by reducing their academic demands.

Although the social and academic dimensions of schooling need not conflict, redesigning our schools for the next century requires us to think about how they work separately and jointly to influence student learning. Using the concepts of *academic press* and *sense of community* to represent these two contrasting normative dimensions, this chapter examines these separate and joint effects. We argue that strong academic press serves as a prerequisite for creating the type of communality in schools that is conducive to higher student achievement.

To test this assertion, we used NELS:88-94 first follow-up data to create measures of school academic press and sense of community. Based on these measures and other key variables, this chapter explores three main hypotheses. First, we expect academic press to have a significant positive impact on student achievement. Second, we expect school sense of community to serve mainly as an amplifier of a school's emphasis -- or lack of emphasis -- on academic goals. In other words, when academic press is strong, sense of community will contribute to student achievement. When it is weak or absent, strong communality will reinforce the pursuit of non-academic goals, thereby inhibiting student achievement. Third, and most important, we expect these various effects to be most conspicuous among schools serving large, socioeconomically disadvantaged student populations. In other words, academic press will have its strongest achievement effect, and sense of community its strongest amplifying effect, in low-SES schools.

One final goal of this chapter is to identify more explicitly the elements of academic press related to output-driven school design. In other words, many of the separate items used to construct the academic press index reflect school and faculty sensitivity to externally generated standards and incentives. Therefore, after gauging the global impact of academic press on student math achievement, we "disentangle" the concept so as to gauge the separate achievement effects of these specific items.

Framing the Research Problem

Academic Press

The term "academic press" typically refers to the degree to which school organizations are driven by achievement oriented values, goals, and norms. Although the term has been used to characterize the pressures students, families, and communities place upon schools (Pace and Stern 1958), its more recent use refers to the normative emphasis schools and teachers place on academic excellence (McDill, Natriello and Pallas 1986), or to other organizational characteristics that help reinforce the value of intellectual effort and performance. Citing it as an essential characteristic of "effective schools," Murphy and his colleagues (Murphy et al. 1982) argue that academic press develops as schools raise their expectations for students, assume responsibility for students' learning, and adopt specific policies and practices.

Some aspects of this framework seem somewhat problematic. For example, even expectations are important, they are not the same as standards; one can imagine teachers holding the high expectation that "all students will learn," while performance standards are continually watered down. Questions also surround the notion of "staff responsibility for student learning." Academic learning is certainly the shared responsibility of students and parents, as well as teachers. Although there may always be room for more effective teaching, assigning academic responsibility primarily to teachers would appear to represent a shifting of responsibility away from students and parents. Finally, while formal policies are suggestive of a school's academic orientation, by themselves they may provide only a superficial portrait of school life.

Despite these problems, the work of Murphy and his colleagues represents an important step in identifying the underpinnings of academically effective school organizations. At the same time, the present analysis seeks to delve deeper, beyond formal descriptions of school environments, and into the small societies that give them life. Envisioning the concept of academic press calls on us to examine how values are expressed in school society, not just in terms of stated goals and standards, but also in terms of the beliefs and behaviors of school members.

Because schools impart values to their members in many different ways, academic press can be reasonably represented by numerous sets of school characteristics. The three components described below summarize one way of thinking about academic press, and constitute the basis of our statistical measures.

Academic Climate. Rather than dispersing their students across a wide range of subjects and ability levels, schools with high academic press channel them into higher status courses such as geometry or physics, rather than consumer math or general science (Oakes 1985). They not only encourage students to work for high grades, but also strive to protect the integrity of the grades they reward. Finally, they emphasize the value of homework and recognize and honor outstanding performance (see Good and Brophy 1986, for a summary of relevant studies).

Disciplinary Climate. A deep understanding exists in schools with high academic press, that broad-based student achievement cannot occur without good attendance, reasonable decorum in hallways and classrooms, or the overall maintenance of a "safe, orderly environment" (Hallinger and Murphy 1986). To that end, such schools work to establish appropriate and effective attendance and disciplinary policies, producing results that are clearly perceived by adult and student school members.

Teachers' Instructional Practices and Emphasis. Teachers express a sense of academic press to the extent that they establish *objective and challenging* standards for student performance; that they cover course content in ways which promote student understanding and desire to learn more; and that they regularly assign meaningful homework and provide useful feedback to students and their parents (see Rutter et al. 1979; McDill, Natriello and Pallas 1986).

A school society marked by high academic press sends strong messages to its members. It informs their activities with purpose, continually signaling that intellectual activities really matter. The principles embodied in the idea of academic press contribute to a school's institutional identity, distinguishing it from, and elevating it to, other character shaping institutions, such as the family, the church, or the Boy Scouts.

The School as a Community

While Communalist understandings run throughout our educational history, visions of "the school as community" have varied greatly in the extent to which they carried any clear sense of academic ethos. For example, Waller's (1932 [1967]) "we feeling" suggests a rugged, traditional vision of community, arising out of competition and shared ordeal. Dewey's (1943 [1956]) "embryonic community" represents a more progressivist, constructivist vision, yet also a somewhat traditional one in its purpose of channeling students along a common, rigorous learning path. Some later understandings, such as Kohlberg's (1980) "just community" and Lightfoot's (1983) "good high school," seem less interested in channeling students than in simply managing their diversity. The so-called "shopping mall" high school in many ways represents the culmination of this vision. After all, it is a place where "pluralism is celebrated as a supreme institutional value," where tolerating diversity is the "moral glue" holding the school together, and where "community" signifies peaceful coexistence rather than common purposeful activity (Powell, Farrar and Cohen 1985).

Several more recent studies, however, conceive of school communality quite differently, in terms of "respect for authority," "consistent enforcement of norms" (Cohen 1983), and as requiring the type of moral and intellectual attitudes, practices, and ideals that evolve when adults refuse to "leave their values at the school door" (Grant 1988). Such visions reflect a more traditional appreciation of schooling's academic mission, calling to mind Rodriguez's (1982) sentiment that the purpose of education is to shape and change young people, rather than to merely accept and accommodate their individual differences and interests.

Bryk and Driscoll (1988) and Bryk, Lee, and Holland (1993) argue that this sort of shaping process is most likely to grow from a particular form of organizational structure. "Communally organized schools," they suggest, evidence the following three core components: (1) a set of shared and commonly understood values among members of the organization, reflected in beliefs about institutional purpose, what students should learn, how adults and students should behave, and students' potential as learners and citizens; (2) a common agenda of activities that define school membership, foster meaningful social interactions among school members, and link them to school traditions; and (3) a distinctive pattern of social relations embodying an ethic of caring visible in both collegial and student-teacher relationships. Together, these components heighten the level and quality of teacher-student engagement, and in turn promote and sustain the school's academic mission.

Implicit within Bryk and Driscoll's work is an understanding of the importance of the academic mission. The "common agenda" implies a narrowing of curricular options toward more traditional academic subjects. The importance of academic orientation is more explicit in Bryk, Lee, and Holland's (1993) study of Catholic schools. Their findings clearly reveal how strong communal organizations, when centered around core academic values, can greatly improve student engagement and achievement.

The Academic and Social Context of Community Building

The previous sentence suggests that the impact of community building might vary greatly depending on how much value school members attach to academic endeavor and accomplishment. Not all schools place high achievement at the top of their normative agenda, and even schools that do must wrestle with a number of academically erosive forces. A longstanding body of literature indicates, for example, the tremendous power of student sub-culture to draw teachers away from objective standards of achievement (Waller 1932 [1967]; Gordon 1957; Coleman 1961; Bidwell 1965). In a similar vein, more recent studies reveal how teachers often apply less stringent criteria to the efforts of "low-ability" minority students (Powell, Farrar and Cohen 1985), or of those viewed as "indifferent, disengaged, or defiant" (Sedlak et al. 1986). It thus becomes apparent how a school's sense of community, if based mainly around social agreement and cohesion, could lose much of its academic underpinning.

More troubling is the likelihood that such forms of community would tend to emerge in schools serving disadvantaged students. Raising student achievement can be an extremely frustrating and daunting task within such schools, and shared norms often reflect a consensus that students are incapable of serious academic effort. For administrators and teachers hesitant to risk the discomfort involved in truly pressing students to achieve, "community building" can amount to a shift toward less risky and, in the short run, more rewarding student outcomes; e.g., friendliness, self-esteem, good citizenship, etc. As communal norms become neutral or even antithetical with respect to achievement, students will more likely experience education that is socially therapeutic, rather than academically challenging. From the standpoint of increasing educational equity across socioeconomic categories, such a tendency should be of tremendous concern.

Note that we are not arguing against efforts to establish stronger, more cohesive communities within disadvantaged schools. We do suggest, however, that the concept of academic press represents a crucial dimension to any meaningful understanding of the school as a community. We also argue that an awareness of this academic dimension is most critical in schools serving disadvantaged students. It is, therefore, among such schools where we expect efforts to strengthen academic press to have their strongest impact on student achievement.

The basis for this argument lies in the fact that academic press can be thought of as a form of social capital, and its value should increase with the scarcity of other academically oriented support structures outside the school. For more affluent students, such alternative resources are often available. Their families are more likely to be intact, and older family members are more likely to have attained higher levels of education. The same is also more likely to be true for family friends, neighbors, and other members of the local community. The resulting network of experience, access, and expectation "presses" students toward higher achievement. The school is part of this network, of course, but as its academic mission is externally reinforced, a form of redundancy exists which makes its contribution less critical. In contrast, the social capital available to less affluent schools may underemphasize or actually undercut the value of academic effort. Those academic support networks which do exist may be weakened by a lack of closure (Coleman and Hoffer 1987). For example, parents have a far more difficult time persuading their teenagers to spend evenings indoors working on homework when other neighborhood teens are allowed to spend unsupervised evening time out on the streets. Such circumstances heighten the importance of whatever academic press the school can provide.

A Direction for Research

A firm basis exists for expecting that achievement stems not simply from consensus, cohesion, and good feeling, but from the strength of specific organizational values and norms. Without a commitment to intellectual endeavor, shared beliefs, common activities, and caring relationships are unlikely to raise (and in some cases may impede) student achievement. At the same time, however, it follows that where meaningful academic commitment exists, these types of communal characteristics should greatly reinforce and contribute to that commitment. Thus, the consequences for educational equity across socioeconomic levels appear to run in two directions. On one hand, we have noted the serious obstacles that can inhibit the development of academically focused communality in low-SES schools. On the other hand, this combination of characteristics may hold significant promise for narrowing the achievement gap across socioeconomic categories.

To summarize the goals and hypotheses presented earlier in this chapter, we intend to measure the separate and interactive impact of school academic press and sense of community using data from NELS:88-94. We expect school academic press to have a positive impact on student math achievement, especially among low-SES schools. Moreover, we expect to see important interactive effects between school academic press, communality, and mean SES. For example, high levels of school communality will likely constrain student achievement in low-SES schools with weak academic press. In contrast, when academic press is high, increased communality should produce even stronger achievement effects.

Methodology

Index Construction

To construct suitable indices of academic press and communality, appropriate items were identified and selected from the NELS:88-94 first follow-up survey. The academic press index was developed based on the theoretical components described earlier in this chapter: academic climate, disciplinary climate, and teachers' instructional practices and emphasis. The communality index, patterned after that previously developed by Bryk and Driscoll (1988) using High School & Beyond data, also comprises three theoretical components: shared values, common agenda, and ethos of caring. (See Appendix 4.1 for general descriptions and technical details of index construction.)

Analytic Design

Equipped with these measures, we examined the achievement effects of academic press and communality in two stages. The first of these utilized a series of hierarchical linear models (HLM) to sort out base effects of these two characteristics and to obtain a preliminary sense of their interactive effects across schools varying in average socioeconomic status. By separating the total variation in student math achievement into within school and between school components, hierarchical modeling allows more precise estimation of "mixed level" or "nested" effects, such as those involving students and schools (see Bryk and Raudenbush 1992). As shall become clearer in the "Results" section later in this chapter, the effects of within school variables (race, track placement, etc.) are presented in a "level-1 equation." The effects of between school variables (academic press, school mean SES, etc.) are presented in a "level-2 equation." (See Appendix 4.2 for descriptions of variables used in this analysis. See Appendix 4.4 for technical details surrounding our HLM analyses.)

The basic strategy for revealing achievement effects using HLM is similar to that which one might use in an ordinary least squares regression. After controlling for pertinent student and school characteristics, variables of direct interest -- in this case, measures of academic press and communality -- are introduced and evaluated.

In the second stage of our analysis, we use a more sophisticated HLM model to uncover and highlight the important three-way interactions which we have predicted should occur among academic press, communality, and school SES. Essentially, this technique involves using continuously coded interaction terms to predict the average math achievement scores that would appear in typical schools exhibiting different combinations of these three variables.

A final set of analyses aims at establishing some connections between schools as output-driven organizations and as organizations whose task it is to convey a sense of academic press to their members. Here, we will identify the elements of academic press reflecting specific qualities of output-driven schools and separately measure their achievement effects.

Source of the Data

This analysis is based on a sub-sample of 398 schools and 7,867 students from the NELS:88-94 first follow-up. Schools were selected on the basis of having at least 15 sampled students and 5 sampled teachers. In addition, because interest centers on "typical" high schools, this sub-sample excludes vocational and boarding schools, as well as schools with 30% or more of their students placed in remedial reading or "alternative school" programs. Although this strategy does not guarantee a statistically representative sample of students, teachers, or schools, exploratory comparisons with the entire first follow-up sample indicate little or no evidence of any systematic bias. The final sample contains an average of 20 students and 11 teachers for each of the 398 schools.

Selection of Dependent Variable

The achievement effects reported here are based on NELS:88-94 first follow-up student mathematics test scores. As noted earlier, the NELS:88-94 data include test scores in history, mathematics, reading, and science, as well as a composite score based on all four of these. While all test scores are moderately to highly correlated, good reasons exist for using the mathematics test. First, because it contained the greatest number of items and ability-level versions, it is arguably the most immune to ceiling and floor effects. Second, math scores reflect *in-school* learning to a greater degree than do other scores.

Results

As indicated earlier, our main research questions concerned the separate and joint effects of school academic press and sense of community across different socioeconomic contexts. Table 4.1 begins to address these questions by revealing the base effects of school mean SES, academic press, and communality. In this hierarchical model, the top panel reports school-level effects; the bottom panel reports the student-level effects, which serve mainly as controls. The coefficients can be interpreted like those in an ordinary multiple regression model; that is, they represent the expected unit change in the dependent variable for each unit change in a particular independent variable.

The bottom, student-level panel of Table 4.1 lists six important background and contextual controls. These particular variables were included because they represent characteristics widely regarded as predictive of student achievement, and because they were significant predictors within this particular student sample. These controls are important for three reasons. First, they help ensure that student-level effects are not improperly attributed to schools. For example, leaving out controls for track placement (VOTRACK and ACTRACK), math course taking (MATHCT), and prior achievement (BY2XMIRR) would blur the issue of whether "academic press" was simply a result of the distribution of talented students across schools. Second, they help ensure that the effects reported for academic press reflect the experience of a typical "general track" student of average ability and social background, who has taken an average number of mainstream mathematics courses. Finally, these controls allow greater confidence that the effects reported for academic press and communality are reasonably pervasive, and not limited to certain types of students.

In the top, or school level panel, of Table 4.1, variables representing school mean SES, academic press, and sense of communality are presented in stepwise fashion across three columns. The first column of coefficients in Table 4.1 reveals the significant effect of a school's average socioeconomic status on student math achievement. Specifically, a one unit difference in school mean SES (MEANSES) is associated with nearly a one unit (.92) difference in student math achievement. (In this analysis, each

TABLE 4.1 Base Effects of School Mean SES, Communality, and Academic Press on Student Mathematics Achievement

Variable	Coeff.	Coeff.	Coeff.
School-level Effects			
MEANSES	.92***	.81***	.56***
COMM		.24*	.09
PRESS			.52***
Student-level Effects			
SES	.43***	.43***	.43***
MINOR	-.91***	-.91***	-.99***
VOTRACK	-1.07***	-1.08***	-1.08***
ACTRACK	1.35***	1.34***	1.30***
MATHCT	1.12***	1.13***	1.13***
BY2XMIRR	.72***	.72***	.72***

* = significant at .05 level; ** = significant at .01 level; *** = significant at .001 level

"point" or "unit" of math achievement represents one correct response on the NELS:88-94 mathematics test.)   The second column of Table 4.1 indicates that school sense of community (COMM) also has a modest significant achievement effect, with each unit of communality tied to a quarter point (.24) difference in student math achievement.   The importance of academic press is evident in the final column of Table 4.1, with each unit linked to about a half point (.52) difference in math achievement. Just as noteworthy as these direct effects is the pattern of interaction revealed across the three columns of Table 4.1. Specifically, academic press appears to account for nearly the entire effect of sense of community and, by implication, well over a third of the effect of school mean SES. The pattern not only suggests that academic press serves as a contextual "linchpin" for school sense of community, but also that part of the socioeconomic achievement gap between schools results from the tendency of more affluent schools to have higher levels of academic press.[1] In fact, the coefficients in the final column of Table 4.1 indicate that in terms of impact on math achievement, one unit of academic press is roughly equivalent to one unit of school-mean SES.

Overall, the results from Table 4.1 clearly indicate the pivotal role of academic press in raising student math achievement. They suggest that previous studies attributing strong achievement effects to communality may have misidentified to some extent the primary source of these effects. Still to be explored, however, is the rather complex pattern of interaction among academic press, sense of community, and school mean SES. Specifically, we suggested earlier that the impact of school communality on student achievement would hinge on the strength of school academic press, and that this relationship would be most evident among low-SES schools.

A preliminary way of checking for these predicted interactions involves the use of dummy-coded interaction terms. For example, we refer to the effect of academic press in low-SES schools as a "two-way" interaction. To examine such effects, we first identify "low-SES" schools, defining them as those schools falling at least one standard deviation below the mean. These schools are assigned a value of "1" for a new variable called LSES, while all other schools are assigned a value of "0" for this new variable. An additional term is then created, a "two-way interaction term," which is simply the product of PRESS and LSES. For moderate and high SES schools, this interaction term will simply equal zero. For low-SES schools, it will equal the school's level of academic press. When this interaction term is inserted into a regression equation (along with its two constituents, LSES and PRESS), its coefficient represents the *additional* effect (either positive or negative) of academic press in low-SES schools beyond its overall effect in *all* schools. A similar procedure is used to observe the effect of academic press in high-SES schools. The same idea can also be used to examine three-way interactions, although as will be seen, there are more effective ways to reveal such covariance.

Using the procedure described above, Table 4.2 offers a preliminary look at how the effects of academic press and sense of community differ across levels of school affluence. For example, the coefficients associated with the PRESS*LSES and PRESS*HSES represent the additional effect of academic press in low and high-SES schools. The coefficients associated with COMM*LSES and COMM*HSES perform the same function with respect to school sense of community. The other interaction terms contained in Table 4.2 (PRESS*COMM, PRESS*COMM*LSES, and PRESS*COMM* HSES) serve mainly as controls which help highlight the two-way interactive effects. That is, because we suspect that sense of community and academic press interact with each other, we need to control for that interaction in order to tease out the separate effects of either of these variables across levels of school SES.

The most striking result in Table 4.2 is the strong influence of academic press in low-SES schools. When academic press is present in any school, the mathematics performance of students is likely to increase. When academic press is present in low-SES schools the increase in mathematics performance is even greater. In other words, a one unit increase of academic press translates into nearly a two point increase in student math achievement in los-SES schools. Table 4.2 is inconclusive, however, with respect to some of our other arguments. For instance, we have suggested that in low-SES schools, communality may sometimes interfere with achievement, but should also have positive amplifying effects when combined with academic press. Although the direction of the effects (COMM*LSES = -.11; PRESS*COMM*LSES = .53) is consistent with these arguments, neither is statistically significant. At least part of this lack of significance may stem from the fact that Table 4.2 does not address or control for some of the other key interactive effects we have predicted. For example, although Table 4.2 attempts to show how the effect of communality differs across levels of school SES, it does not account for the possibility that this interaction itself might differ across levels of school academic press. To do so using dummy coding would require the inclusion of a number of additional interaction terms, essentially "carving up" the data into a larger number of smaller cells, and disintegrating much of its predictive power.

The second stage of our analysis obtains a clearer picture of the interactions among school SES, academic press, and communality. We accomplish this by deriving hypothetical school types representing different categorical combinations of these three variables (for example, schools with low academic press, high communality, and low-SES; schools with moderate academic press, low communality, and moderate SES, etc.). Twenty-seven combinations of low, medium, and high SES, academic press, and communality can be defined. The median serves as a representative value for each category of each of the three variables. The medians are then substituted into a school-level HLM equation containing continuously coded interaction terms (PRESS*COMM*MEANSES, PRESS*COMM, etc. See Appendix 4.3) to produce a predicted achievement effect for each representative school type.

The three-way interaction among academic press, communal organization, and SES is shown graphically in Figure 4.1, which displays the increment or decrement to a student's predicted math achievement (as represented by the school mean) associated with each hypothetical school type. Each panel of Figure 4.1 represents a school SES category. In each SES category, the expected achievement effect is measured along the vertical axis, and levels of academic press along the horizontal axis, with each line style representing a different level of communality. For each category of school SES, this configuration reveals the predicted effects of

TABLE 4.2 Interactive Achievement Effects of Academic Press, Communality, and School SES

Variable	Coeff
School-level Effects	
MEANSES	.80**
COMM	.21
PRESS	.55**
LSES	.40
HSES	-.43
PRESS*LSES	1.22*
PRESS*HSES	-.10
COMM*LSES	-.11
COMM*HSES	.37
PRESS*COMM	.09
PRESS*COM*LSES	.53
PRESS*COMM*HSES	-.46
Student-level Effects	
SES	.43**
MINOR	-.99***
VOTRACK	-1.08***
ACTRACK	1.31***
MATHCT	1.13***
BY2XMIRR	.72***

* = significant at .05 level; ** = significant at .01 level; *** = significant at .001 level

academic press at a given level of communality, and those of communality at a given level of academic press.

Striking evidence supporting the main arguments of this chapter is found in the first panel of Figure 4.1, which represents low-SES schools. Here, the rising slopes of each line indicate the positive impact of academic press at all levels of communality. For example, among highly communal schools (represented by the solid black line), those with high academic press are expected to attain levels of math achievement about four points higher than those with low academic press. A similar, smaller advantage is apparent among low and moderately communal schools. In contrast, by scanning the vertical distance between the lines at each level of academic press, one sees how the direction of the communality effect depends on the level of school academic press. Among schools with low academic press, for instance, those with high communality produce math achievement levels about one point lower than those with low communality. The impact of communality among low-SES schools becomes positive, however, as levels of academic press increase. In fact, the strongest achievement effects among low-SES schools occur when both communality and academic press are at their highest levels.

For low-SES schools, a strong academic context serves as a prerequisite for communality's positive achievement effects. A similar pattern is seen in the center panel of Figure 4.1, which represents medium-SES schools. As in the first panel, academic press has positive effects at all levels of communality and the strongest achievement effect is predicted for schools with high combined levels of both variables. In contrast to low-SES schools, however, no negative effects are predicted at any level of communality. Shifting to the final panel, the pattern seems to be reversed for high-SES schools. The impact of academic press begins to fade among highly communal schools, and in fact, math achievement appears to be more related to communality than academic press.

The contrasting patterns revealed in Figure 4.1 across school SES levels serve as an exclamation point to the pattern of statistical findings revealed previously. They suggest that by increasing their academic press, low-SES schools may attain levels of achievement approaching those of their middle and high SES counterparts. The potential for such improvement is even stronger when high academic press is coupled with a strong set of communal norms.

Examining the Output-Driven Elements of Academic Press

Whether a response to direct local incentives or to more diffuse national demands for higher achievement, academic press represents an indication of school "output-drivenness." Specifically, however, our academic press index contains numerous individual items representing school characteristics more directly tied to this concept (see Appendix 4.1). Table 4.3 lists, describes, and presents the univariate effects of eight such variables reflecting school sensitivity to either external demands for, or objective standards of, student performance. For example, course requirements in foreign language (F1C70G) and channeling students into "mainstream" academic courses (S11 and S12) signify a school's sensitivity to parental demand or to college entrance requirements. Honoring and publicizing achievement (F1C91F) signifies the extent to which student academic performance is valued in the school community.

FIGURE 4.1 Predicted Interactive Achievement Effects of Academic Press, Communality, and School SES

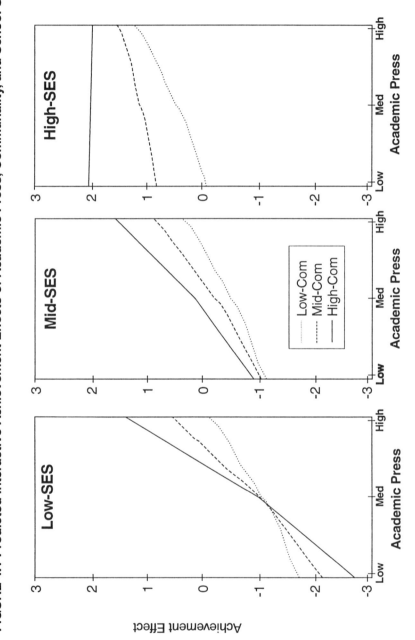

TABLE 4.3 Indicators of Output-Driven School Organization

Variable	Description [a]	Range [b]	Univariate Achievement Effect [c]
T1	Teachers notify parents of poor student	4.89	.54***
GRDCRIT	Teachers emphasize absolute achievement	8.04	.27*
F1C70G	Number of years required in foreign	4.77	.59***
F1C70B	Number of years required in math	6.74	.05
S11	Student course taking in mainstream	5.47	.52***
S12	Student course taking in mainstream	5.95	.48***
F1C91F	School honors & publicizes high	5.04	.15
F1C93D	Teachers press students to achieve	4.31	.54***

[a] For more detailed variable descriptions see Appendix *4.1.

[b] Variables standardized to mean=0 and standard deviation=1.

[c] HLM coefficients, student-level controls identical to those in Table *4.2.
* = significant at .05 level; ** = significant at .01 level; *** = significant at .001 level.

The univariate coefficients shown in Table 4.3 reveal significant positive achievement effects for six of the eight output-driven characteristics: teachers notifying parents regarding their child's poor performance (T1), teachers emphasizing absolute achievement in grading (GRDCRIT), course requirements in foreign language (F1C70G), student course taking in standard science and humanities (S11 and S12), and the principal's belief that teachers press students to achieve (F1C93D). Although the effect of honoring and publicizing student achievement (F1C91F) is not statistically significant, exploratory analyses revealed significant effects for this variable among low-SES schools. The weak effect of math course taking is no surprise, considering the wide content and ability range of courses often available to students. For example, one might not expect an additional year of consumer math to greatly raise a student's math achievement. This weak effect may also indicate a tendency of low achieving schools to have recently increased their math course requirements.

Presenting the multivariate effects associated with these output-driven characteristics, Table 4.4 reveals how they interact with each other and with school mean socioeconomic status. In each of the first four columns, pairs of variables are introduced to represent a different type of school or classroom characteristic. The last column of Table 4.4 introduces a control for school socioeconomic status (MEANSES). Although the changes in significance and magnitude across the columns indicate the covariance among these characteristics, four of them -- teachers contacting parents

TABLE 4.4 Effects of "Output-Driven" Characteristics on 10th Grade Math Achievement[a]

Variable[b]	Teacher Practices	Curricular Policies	Course Taking	Academic Climate	School Affluence
TN	.55***	.48***	.41***	.37**	.25*
GRDCRI	.27*	.21*	.21*	.19*	.10
F1C70B		-.07	-.15	-.16	-.13
F1C70G		.50***	.40**	.38**	.31**
S11			.36**	.32**	.26*
S12			.17	.16	.04
F1C91F				.13	.15
F1C93D				.35**	.28*
MEANS					.47**

[a] HLM coefficients. Student-level controls are identical to Tables 4.1 and 4.2.

[b] Variables are standardized to mean=0 and standard deviation=1.

* = significant at .05 level; ** = significant at .01 level; *** = significant at .001 level

(TN), school foreign language requirements (F1C70G), student course work in mainstream science (S11), and teachers pressing students to achieve (F1C93D) -- retain significant positive effects on math achievement. The pattern of interaction revealed in the final column suggests that the effects of these four output-driven characteristics, while significant for all schools, are partially explained by the fact that they tend to be practiced in more affluent schools. This pattern is similar to that found for school academic press, in the sense that higher-SES schools tend to have higher levels of academic press. The data suggest that the separate characteristics, mentioned above, may produce stronger achievement effects in low-SES schools. While we do not pursue this interaction here, such an analysis would certainly shed further light on how organizational norms and practices can produce differing effects across differing socioeconomic contexts.

Discussion

These findings support the main arguments of this chapter in the following ways: (1) academic press is significantly linked to mathematics achievement, and its strongest effects occur in low-SES schools; (2) for schools at low and middle SES levels, high combined levels of academic press and communality produce a strong achievement effect; (3) for low-SES schools, the combination of weak academic press and strong communality has significant negative impact on math achievement; and (4) for high-SES schools, communality is positively linked to math achievement across all levels of academic press. In addition, our findings reveal how specific "output-driven" elements of academic press contribute to student achievement.

In a far broader sense, our findings reveal vital connections among academic excellence, educational equity, and output-drivenness. It seems unfortunate that words like "excellence" and "standards" are sometimes misunderstood by policy makers, and often viewed as codewords for educational exclusivity and inequality. Yet, these results indicate that increased sensitivity to academic incentives and the need for higher achievement standards actually serve to promote greater educational equity across school socioeconomic levels. In other words, as schools become more output-driven, they also become better able to generate among their members the type of normative social current necessary for meaningful academic success.

Still, with regard to educational equity, some argue that it would be unreasonable to expect all schools to hold similarly high standards until all schools receive similar levels of fiscal resources. Our findings, however, indicate that much variation exists in the degree to which even low-SES schools "press" their students to achieve, and that much of that variation is directly tied to differences in the way these schools apply their human and social resources toward academic goals. While fiscal resources will always be important, it would seem that policy makers may be overlooking a more serious type of inequity in public education; that is, the unequal distribution of academically oriented norms and incentives across socioeconomic levels.

Establishing and maintaining the type of norms and incentives that lead to higher levels of student learning has become an increasingly crucial problem for schools. In many schools today, even in those serving more affluent families and communities, students often gain status among their peers by avoiding any appearance of interest in academic work. Unfortunately, schools often accommodate such students by watering down academic standards and course requirements or by offering a wide range of non-academic options for disengaged students. Society, too, accommodates students' academic antipathy by constraining the extent to which employers may consider high school grades in hiring decisions, and through a higher education system which enables virtually any student to attend college, regardless of prior academic performance. Thus, in a real sense for many of today's students, what was once a college is now more like a high school, and what was once a high school is now more like a junior high school.

The problem of recapturing the "hearts and minds" of American high schools and the students they serve becomes a crucial challenge. More specifically, schools must find ways to translate the standard script about the importance of academic effort and performance into a day-to-day reality for all students and teachers. Our evidence suggests that most schools--and particularly low-SES schools--can meet this challenge by placing their academic mission at center stage and allowing their social mission to play a supporting role. This sort of organizational casting by no means diminishes the importance of the latter; for around such frameworks as "the school as community' and "the teacher as coach" develops a network of social support through which academic norms can flow and flourish. However, it is key for schools to recognize their fundamental purpose as a transmitter of knowledge and skills. While some would have schools function primarily as something close to a student's "second family," schools, as institutions, are vastly different from families. They are born, not out of love and personal attachment, but out of the individual's need for learning and society's need for educated citizens. From such understandings grow the meaningful attachments and relationships we typically associate with the schooling experience.

Recognizing and highlighting their academic mission not only allows schools to maintain their identity and integrity as institutions, but also provides the critical context for the care, concern, and support they need to offer their students. As evidenced by the strong achievement effects we found when low-SES schools center their community building efforts around the core of academic press, such attention to context pays off in the form of higher student achievement.

Notes

1. Comparisons of academic press levels across school socioeconomic level (not tabulated here), in fact, indicate this tendency.

Appendix 4.1

Index Construction

The indices of academic press and communality consist of items selected or constructed from NELS:88-94 data. The academic press index comprises 28 items (Cronbach's alpha = .73), and the communality index of 24 (Cronbach's alpha = .84). In the outlines below, item names beginning with F1C, F1T, or F1S are from the Principal, Teacher, or Student survey, respectively. Other names (e.g., S1, ACCLIM, or KENW) represent composite variables. Items were standardized (mean = 0, sd = 1) prior to inclusion in an overall index.

Academic Press Index

Academic Climate
ACCLIM: Factor composite of F1C93C (class activities highly structured), F1C93D (teachers press students to achieve), F1C93E (students expected to do homework), F1C93I (students encouraged to compete for grades), and F1C93J (students encouraged to enroll in academic classes). Factor loadings: F1C93C, .72; F1C93D, .86; F1C93E, .81; F1C93I, .55; F1C93J, .75. Eigenvalue = 2.78.)

F1C91F: Degree to which school publicizes and honors student achievement.

F1C70B, F1C70G: Number of semesters required in math and foreign language.

MA: School percent of teachers with masters degree or higher (F1C35, F1C44C, F1C44D).

S11: School mean semesters in biology, chemistry, or physics (F1S23C, F1S23E, F1S23G).

S12: School mean semesters in history, geography, or foreign language (F1S24B, F1S24C, F1S24D, F1S24G).

S1: School mean agreement that "teaching is good" (F1S7G).

S18: School mean agreement that high school courses "were harder" than prior courses (F1S65A).

Disciplinary Climate
F1C24: Number of absences allowed before student considered truant (reversed scale).

F1C102A: Principal reported frequency at which parents are notified of student absences.

F1C102C: Frequency at which parents are notified if student is sent to office.

S4: School mean student disagreement that "disruptions by other students impede my learning" (F1S7N).

S5: School mean student disagreement that "misbehaving students often get away with it" (F1S7O).

S6: School percent of students perceiving that when last absent, the "school did not do anything" (F1S15A converted to dichotomous variable; equals 1 if "no," i.e., school did something; equals 0 if "yes" or "don't know," i.e., school did nothing or student didn't know if school did anything).

T23: School mean disagreement that tardiness and class cutting interfere with teaching (F1T4_1M).

T10: School mean disagreement that student misbehavior outside class interferes with teaching (F1T4_1E).

Teachers' Instructional Practices and Emphasis
GRDCRIT: Factor composite of influence of "absolute level of achievement" in teachers' grading decisions (F1T3_24A) compared to that of "achievement relative to class" (F1T3_24B), "participation" (F1T3_24E), and "attendance" (F1T3_24G). Factor loadings: F1T3_24A, .34; F1T3_24B, .33; F1T3_24E, .80; and F1T3_24 G, .81. Eigenvalue= 1.52.

T21: School mean degree to which "cover the curriculum" is most important teaching goal (F1T4_11B).

T24: School mean degree to which "understand subject matter" is most important teaching goal (F1T4_11C).

T22: School mean degree to which "create lessons students will enjoy" is most important teaching goal (F1T4_11F).

T6: School mean amount of homework assigned per week (F1T2_9H, F1T2_9M).

T2: School mean of how often teachers discuss completed assignments with students (F1T2_10C).

T1: School percent of teachers giving a consistent response to items F1T1_2 (student usually works hard) and F1T1_6A (spoken to parents about student performance).

T3: School mean time spent per week planning and preparing for teaching (F1T323AH, F1T323AM).

T4: School mean time spent per week correcting student work (F1T323BH, F1T323BM).

S13: School mean of how often students say they are asked to show they "really understand" the lesson in math, English, history, and science (F1S26A, F1S26B, F1S26C, F1S26D). For responses to be included in the construction of this measure, students had to be taking at least two of these subjects.

S14: School mean of how often students say they feel "challenged" in math, English, history, and science (F1S26A, F1S26B, F1S26C, F1S26D). For responses to be included in the construction of this measure, students had to be taking at least two of these subjects.

School Communality Index

Shared Values
KENW: Kendall's "W" for rankings of the following: F1T4_11B (cover curriculum), F1T4_11C (understand subject matter), F1T4_11D (perform well on tests), F1T4_11E (maintain order and discipline), F1T4_11F (enjoy learning), and F1T4_11G (employment skills).

T12: School mean agreement that "goals and priorities for the school are clear" (F1T4_1J).

T9: School mean agreement that "colleagues share my beliefs about school mission" (F1T4_1C).

T18: School mean agreement that "rules for student behavior are consistently enforced" (F1T4_2L).

T16: School mean perception of "broad agreement among faculty about school mission" (F1T4_2F).

T11: School mean disagreement that "students are incapable of learning the material" (F1T4_1I).

F1C93M: Principal's perception of "much conflict between teachers and administrators" (reversed scale).

F1C93K: Principal's perception that "teachers have a negative attitude about students" (reversed scale).

Common Agenda of Activities
TSPREAD: Based on student and principal reports, let p1, p2, and p3, respectively, represent the percentage of students in the vocational, general, and academic tracks; then TSPREAD represents the student/principal average of the reversed scale natural log of p1(1-p1) + p2(1-p2) + p3(1-p3).

S22_24S: School sum of standard deviations of variables S10, S11, and S12. S10 represents the school mean number of semesters taken by students in algebra I (F1S22C), geometry (F1S22D), algebra II (F1S22E), and/or trigonometry (F1S22F). (For descriptions of S11 and S12, see above).

S15: School percent of student sample participating in school sports (F1S41AA - F1S41AH).

S16: School percent of student sample participating in other extracurricular activities (F1S41BA - F1S41BI).

S17: School percent of student sample in leadership roles in sports or other extracurricular activities (F1S41AA- F1S41BI).

Organizational Characteristics
T19: School mean agreement that department colleagues helped them improve their teaching (F1T4_8D).

T20: School mean agreement that colleagues outside department helped them improve their teaching (F1T4_8E).

T7: School mean report of coordination of course content within department (F1T4_1A).

T14: School mean report of coordination of course content between departments (F1T4_1N).

T8: School mean agreement that "you can count on other staff members to help out" (F1T4_1B).

T15: School mean agreement that "there is a great deal of cooperative effort among staff members" (F1T4_2E).

T5: School mean weekly time spent meeting with other teachers (F1T323CH, F1T323CM).

T13: School mean disagreement that the "staff seldom evaluates its programs" (F1T4_1K).

T17: School mean agreement that "school seems like one big family" (F1T4_2H).

S2: School mean agreement that "teachers are interested in students as people" (F1S7H).

S3: School mean agreement that "most teachers really listen to what I have to say" (F1S7L).

Appendix 4.2

TABLE 4.A.1 Descriptive Statistics

Student Variables	Description	Mean	S.D.	Range
F1TXMIRR	Dependent variable; 10th grade math achievement, IRT score	38.17	12.25	46.87
SES	Student socioeconomic status	0.10	0.79	5.71
MINOR	1 if Black or Hispanic	0.17	0.37	1.00
VOTRACK	1 if in vocational program	0.14	0.34	1.00
ACTRACK	1 if in academic program	0.37	0.48	1.00
BY2XMIRR	8th grade math achievement, IRT score	24.02	8.65	32.65
MATHCT	Number of math courses taken, algebra and beyond	2.96	1.94	8.00
School Variables	Description	Mean	S.D.	Range
MEANSES	School-mean SES	0.00	1.00	5.81
LSES	1 if in low MEANSES category	0.14	0.34	1.00
MSES	1 if in mid MEANSES category	0.71	0.46	1.00
HSES	1 if in high MEANSES category	0.16	0.37	1.00
COMM	Communality index	0.00	1.00	6.14
PRESS	Academic press index	0.00	1.00	6.06

Appendix 4.3

Table 4.A.2 summarizes the HLM equation used to derive the effects shown in Figure 4.1. (Because the student-level equation is virtually identical to those presented in Table 4.1 and Table 4.2, it is not included here.) It should be noted that these effects relate not to cells or cell sizes, but to relative differences between continuous values of academic press, communality, and school-mean SES within and among schools in the sample. The predicted effects are thus *independent* of actual sample distribution across the 18 hypothetical school categories.

TABLE *4.A.2 Interactive Effects of School-mean SES (MEANSES), Academic Press (PRESS), and Communal Organization (COMM)

Variable	Coefficient
MEANSES	.71***
COMM	.26
PRESS	.66***
MEANSES*COMM*PRESS	-.16*
MEANSES*PRESS	-.25
MEANSES*COMM	.15
PRESS*COMM	.09

* = significant at .05 level; ** = significant at .01 level; *** = significant at .001 level

Appendix 4.4

Technical Details

Important descriptive and technical issues arose in this analysis which could not be succinctly integrated into the text. Although space does not permit an in-depth treatment of these issues (see Shouse 1994, for full technical details), highlighted here are details related to model specification and proportion of variance explained.

Model Specification

In specifying a student-level model, one must consider not only the estimate of student-level effects, but also whether these effects vary significantly across schools. Statistics provided by the HLM program can reveal such cross-level covariance, thus facilitating reasonable specification decisions. When no significant cross-level covariance is found for a given variable, the error variance can be fixed to zero and the variable centered around its grand mean. If significant covariance is found, the variance may be estimated for each school and the variable centered around the school mean. Failing to appropriately address such cross-level covariance can lead to mis-estimates of school-level effects.

In this analysis, statistics indicated significant cross-school variation in two of the six student variables: vocational track placement (VOTRACK) and math course taking (MATHCT). These were treated as random and centered around their school means. Thus, for the hierarchical models presented in this chapter, the intercept would represent a predicted student achievement level weighted for differences in the degree of track placement and math course taking across schools, much in the same way as if school-level measures of these effects had been included in the school-level model.

Proportion of Variance Explained

Based on statistics provided by the HLM program, it is estimated that the variation in student achievement breaks down to about 80% within schools and 20% between schools. The six student-level variables account for roughly 71% of the within school variation. The proportion of between school variance explained ranges from about 17% (Table 1) to about 25% (Table 2).

5

Reconsidering Roles and Incentives in Schools

Stephen Plank, Huayin Wang, and Barbara Schneider

External Standards as Incentives for Achievement

This chapter examines the relationship between external standards for performance, and student achievement in mathematics and science. There are several advantages to linking external standards, assessments, and rewards to educators rather than simply to students. In Chapter 2, we argue that external standards can help establish school and classroom norms that promote achievement. Further, externally set standards can relieve the conflict teachers encounter when they are placed in the disparate roles of both standard setter and coach.

There are some risks inherent in relying on external performance standards. Some researchers have suggested that such standards will ultimately result in further corrupting testing practices that are already culturally biased and will serve to decrease rather than increase equality of educational opportunity (Apple 1993). Others have cautioned that we should not focus on standards and tests as educational panaceas so exclusively that we lose sight of the large inequities that exist in students' opportunities for learning at local school sites (Darling-Hammond 1994).

We take these risks seriously but believe that efforts can be made to overcome cultural bias and inequitable opportunities to learn. We must not, however, overlook the considerable potential of performance standards as a motivating force that can energize educators and students by focusing their actions on improving achievement. The analyses in this chapter are prompted by the hypothesis that external standards can have a direct effect on student performance. Additionally, we expect that external standards may affect academic performance indirectly through specific school-level policies and teachers' practices in classrooms.

The American educational system has been criticized for being administratively-driven. That is, it has been described as being too bureaucratic in its organization and as operating in a manner that does little to encourage the efforts of teachers or students toward high levels of learning. We suspect that both the absence of external standards for performance, and the lack of incentives for teachers and students to meet such standards, have created social systems in many schools and districts that place little value on high performance or effort. In contrast, output-driven systems in which principals, teachers, and students are evaluated and rewarded on the basis of students' performance on external examinations can fundamentally change how these various actors relate to one another. Well-publicized external criteria of performance from which meaningful consequences flow can counteract norms and values which trivialize academic effort and achievement.

Using the NELS:88-94 base year and first follow-up longitudinal panel, we estimate a series of models that predict gains in mathematics and science achievement between the eighth and tenth grades. The models are intended to test our assumptions about the direct and indirect effects of external standards on student performance in mathematics and science. While the focus is on student achievement, these models are constructed to reflect variation in the roles and incentives for principals and teachers in addition to students. We also maintain that external standards and how they are employed need to be examined in conjunction with actual teacher instructional practices. Therefore, our models also contain measures of specific teaching techniques and curricular emphases in both mathematics and science.

External Standards and Classroom Practices

Two U.S. presidents, the nation's governors, and a sizeable number of legislators have strongly endorsed the goal of U.S. students placing first in the world in science and mathematics performance by the year 2000 (National Education Goals Panel 1991). Despite federal and state support for this goal, some would argue that it is untenable, especially considering how our current educational system is organized. The mathematics and science performance of U.S. students continues to lag behind the performance of students in other industrialized nations (NCEA Research and Development Report 1992). At a national level, periodic results from the National Assessment of Educational Progress (NAEP) show only a modest growth in mathematics and reading skills. Comparisons between national longitudinal cohorts of high school students over the past two decades show that sophomores in 1990 were achieving at slightly higher levels than sophomores in 1980 (Rasinski, Ingels, Rock and Pollack 1993). However, when estimates take into account the increases in parent education, the achievement profiles of the two tenth grade cohorts look quite similar. As we show in Chapter 3, much of the improvement seen between 1980 and 1990 can be explained by increases in the human capital of the family. While the evidence in Chapter 3 cautions us against alarmist opinions concerning the state of education in the U.S., there is still reason to desire stronger academic results from our schools, especially from those institutions that serve students who have traditionally been viewed as at-risk. Poor academic performance continues to be a serious problem in many of these schools. We contend that such poor academic performance can be tied directly to the incentive structures in schools that fail to reward or publicly support academic performance.

Today, many administrators, teachers, and students are rarely held directly accountable for their actions in school. The lack of accountability regarding specific standards of performance creates unclear expectations of behavior. Without external requirements, teachers are placed in roles with conflicting pressures. They are asked to improve students' performance and determine what level of performance is required for a given grade. Students are not unaware of their teachers' predicament, and it is not unusual for students to negotiate with their teachers in order to influence the criteria and scale used for awarding grades. In such situations, high performance standards can easily be compromised in exchange for friendly and orderly classrooms (Sizer 1984). These conditions are likely to diminish the value placed on tasks such as homework, on rewards such as grades, and, ultimately, on achievement.

Roles and Incentives

One of the major concerns regarding American education has been that principals are often seen as having little control over their schools. In large, urban, bureaucratic systems, principals are often described as middle managers who lack autonomy in establishing the standards of performance for both teachers and students at their schools (Wong 1995). When principals are given more direct control of their respective schools by allowing them, for example, to set performance standards, these principals can exercise greater authority over the quality of their own schools (Hallinger and Murphy 1986).

When principals are given more authority and control over their schools, it becomes more reasonable to establish accountability standards of performance. One measure of principal accountability is the evaluation of his or her performance on the basis of student test scores. Such an external measure of performance, we suspect, would encourage the school leader to promote academic achievement norms as well as take measures to ensure that they are met.

Publicizing student test scores by sending them home to parents can serve as a mechanism for making student academic achievement an explicit and legitimate criteria for the principal's evaluation. Distributing test results to parents can also accomplish two other important functions. First, it indicates to parents how well their child is performing in school. Second, it also indicates more indirectly how well the school system is functioning in helping the child perform. Thus, test results can be seen as indicators of the accomplishments of the child, as well as the system's provision of opportunities for that child to learn.

The educational system can regulate opportunities for student learning by delegating to external parties determination of curriculumar content, and by making teachers accountable for covering those topics. Giving teachers too much control over what topics are covered in their classrooms can potentially create severe problems, especially as students move from one teacher to another each year. Specifically, a lack of continuity and teachers' uncertainty about their students' prior exposure to particular topics can arise when there is insufficient coordination of the curriculum.

On the other hand, allowing teachers flexibility in determining what instructional techniques they use in their classrooms can be beneficial. For example, in some instances, as a matter of efficiency, a teacher may be inclined to dedicate instructional time to addressing the whole class rather than working with small groups. In other instances, a teacher may choose to use small groups to encourage student involvement and cooperative learning. By having discretionary authority over instructional practices such as grouping, monitoring student performance, and assignment of homework, teachers can more productively direct their efforts and those of their students toward academic goals. Thus, when control over pedagogical techniques is left largely in the hands of teachers, they are free to find the best ways to maximize their students' performance toward common goals.

Two indicators of student performance in classrooms are test scores and grades. In comparing the two, scores on externally designed tests are not subject to negotiation between teachers and students in the same way grades often are. Thus, test scores can be perceived as fairly objective measures of performance in that they are not influenced by the teachers' assessment of students. Grades, on the other hand, can be subject to relative standards of performance - such as how well a student is doing relative to the rest of the class - or based on criteria not directly tied to achievement - such as good behavior or turning in homework assignments. The relative standards associated with grading practices occur because many teachers are faced with being both the person who sets the grading standards and the person who tries to get students to meet those standards. In holding these two roles, teachers often find themselves in a difficult position because their grading standards can be directly challenged by students and parents. If the standards used to measure performance are not under the teachers' control, students and parents have less reason to bargain over acceptable levels of performance and the criteria for achieving them.

Measuring performance on the basis of absolute achievement is likely to send the tacit message to students that assessment criteria are determined beyond the walls of the classroom. Such a message increases the likelihood that students will not try to haggle and negotiate about performance standards. As a result, this source of conflict between teachers and students is lessened and a common focus on high achievement may be expected. Assuming that external standards affect performance and influence teaching practices, we are interested in the following issues; 1) whether a school's reliance on external standards is positively associated with gains in student achievement, and 2) whether these achievement effects operate through specific teaching practices.

These two issues are explored by examining growth in mathematics and science achievement as measured by the cognitive tests included in NELS:88-94 base year and first follow-up instruments. We deliberately selected mathematics performance because such learning is sensitive to school-related instruction. Furthermore, the hierarchical and sequential organization of the high school mathematics curriculum (Stevenson, Schiller and Schneider 1994) makes standardized test results highly informative, with variation in test score growth being directly linked to variation in school and classroom practices and curricular exposure. Even though the science curriculum in high schools is not as hierarchically organized as the mathematics curriculum, it is more likely to be linked to school-related instruction than other subjects such as English. Competency in English is more difficult to trace to specific practices, since students are expected to write in other subjects such as history.

Data, Measures, and Models

Using weighted data from the first follow-up student panel, and the high school administrator and teacher surveys, we employ multiple regression techniques to estimate the relationship between output-driven factors and growth in mathematics and science performance. In examining the relationship between output-driven organizational factors and individual growth in mathematics and science achievement, we estimate a series of models which isolate the effects of output-driven factors at both the school and classroom levels.

We begin by estimating a baseline model that takes into account student and school factors that other research has consistently shown to influence student achievement. The subsequent models explore the effect of different aspects of output-driven schools on student achievement, beginning with school-level characteristics (such as the dissemination of test scores) and then focusing on teachers' and students' classroom decisions and actions. Our goal is to reveal the degree to which output-driven characteristics, at the various levels of a school's organization, influence student achievement in mathematics and science. The mathematics models are presented in Table 5.1; the science models are presented in Table 5.2.

The baseline model (Model A) for each subject (i.e mathematics and science) includes prior test scores, individual background characteristics, and the type of school attended. To take into account the effects of prior mathematics knowledge, the eighth grade mathematics test score and a squared term for the eighth grade mathematics score are included.[1] The science models, are constructed similarly and contain as independent variables the eighth grade science test score, and a squared term for the eighth grade science score. The science model also includes the eighth grade mathematics score since preliminary analyses showed that success on the science test is partially dependent on a student's basic computational skills. These computational skills are best reflected through the inclusion of the mathematics test results.

Other individual characteristics in the baseline model include race and ethnicity (i.e., Asian American, Hispanic, and African American, with white as the reference category), gender, and a measure of parents' education, which takes one of six levels ranging from less than high school graduation to Ph.D., M.D., or the equivalent. School variables include location (i.e., urban and rural, with suburban as the reference category) and school type (i.e., Catholic, National Association of Independent Schools [NAIS], and other private schools, with public schools as the reference category).

In Model B, we introduce four measures which capture aspects of the school-level organization and mechanisms for achieving principal and teacher accountability. The relative influence of students' test performance on the principal's evaluation is represented by a dummy variable indicating whether students' test scores have at least as much influence on how the principal is evaluated by his or her supervisors as each of three other criteria; 1) the disciplinary environment in the school, 2) efficient administration, and 3) parent or community support. The measures of the principal's influence on hiring teachers and the principal's influence on setting teacher performance standards relate to the principal's authority or

TABLE 5.1 OLS Coefficients for Models of Tenth Grade Mathematics Achievement[a,b]

Variables	Model A	Model B	Model C	Model D	Model E	Model F
Intercept	-5.75***	-6.64***	-8.43***	-7.46***	-5.49***	-6.65***
Eighth grade math test	1.66***	1.66***	1.65***	1.59***	1.49***	1.46***
(Eighth grade math test)^2	-0.01***	-0.01***	-0.01***	-0.01***	-0.01***	-0.01***
Asian American	-0.53	-0.58	-0.58	-0.62	-0.55	-0.46
Hispanic	-1.15**	-1.23**	-1.19**	-1.31**	-1.35***	-1.41***
African American	-2.20***	-2.31***	-2.24***	-2.38***	-2.39***	-2.32***
Male	-0.26	-0.22	-0.17	-0.11	0.03	0.59**
Parents' education	0.88***	0.88***	0.84***	0.76***	0.71***	0.64***
Urban	0.15	0.05	0.02	0.04	-0.11	-0.16
Rural	-0.34	-0.36	-0.25	-0.24	-0.20	-0.27
Catholic	0.96*	1.06**	1.08**	0.66	0.52	0.36
NAIS	0.29	0.50	0.40	0.38	0.28	0.54
Other private	1.23	1.26	1.42*	2.20**	1.80**	1.84**
Relative influence of tests in evaluating principal		0.33	0.30	0.25	0.24	0.29
Principal's influence on hiring teachers		-0.27	-0.26	-0.20	-0.18	-0.13

(continues)

TABLE 5.1 (continued)

Principal's influence on setting teachers' performance standards	0.24	0.25*	0.21	0.22	0.15
Test results sent to parents	0.26*	0.24*	0.24*	0.27**	0.25*
Teacher's control over content		-0.15*	-0.12	-0.16*	-0.19**
Teacher's control over teaching technique		0.41**	0.21	0.34*	0.23
Relative importance of absolute achievement in grading		0.70***	0.61**	0.48*	0.50*
Relative importance of individual improvement in grading		-0.16	-0.04	-0.14	-0.20
Time spent instructing whole class			0.73***	0.60***	0.58***
Time spent instructing small group			-0.13	-0.13	-0.10
Time spent instructing individuals			-0.08	-0.08	-0.06
Time spent maintaining order			-0.39***	-0.26*	-0.19
Teacher keeps records of who turned in assignments			-0.42**	-0.36**	-0.48***
Teacher returns assignments with grades and corrections			0.17	0.16	0.16
Teacher discusses completed assignments in class			0.63***	0.45**	0.48**
Emphasis on understanding the nature of proof				0.80***	0.70***
Emphasis on memorizing facts, rules, and steps				-0.07	-0.10

(continues)

TABLE 5.1 *(continued)*

Emphasis on becoming interested in mathematics					0.18	0.20
Emphasis on importance of mathematics in everyday life					-0.99***	-1.05***
Emphasis on performing computations with speed and accuracy					-0.33*	-0.32*
Emphasis on importance of math in basic and applied sciences					0.65***	0.62***
Student usually works hard for good grades						0.97***
Student often completes homework						0.79***
Student is often disruptive in class						-0.28*
Adjusted R^2	0.775	0.776	0.777	0.782	0.787	0.794

[a] based on 4315 cases for whom questionnaires are available from tenth grade mathematics teachers; weighted by panel weight.

[b] * p<.05; ** p<.01; ***p<.001

TABLE 5.2 OLS Coefficients for Models of Tenth Grade Science Achievement[a,b]

Variables	Model A	Model B	Model C	Model D	Model E	Model F
Intercept	2.04*	0.95	0.11	0.76	-0.27	0.27
Eighth grade science test	0.70***	0.70***	0.71***	0.69***	0.69***	0.64***
(Eighth grade science test)^2	-0.004*	-0.004	-0.005*	-0.004	-0.004	-0.004
Eighth grade math test	0.19***	0.19***	0.18***	0.18***	0.18***	0.17***
Asian American	-0.95**	-0.97**	-0.99**	-0.91**	-0.93**	-0.91**
Hispanic	-0.84***	-0.82**	-0.83**	-0.91***	-0.92***	-0.94***
African American	-1.41***	-1.39***	-1.39***	-1.43***	-1.46***	-1.43***
Male	1.02***	1.01***	1.03***	1.01***	1.03***	1.28***
Parents' education	0.34***	0.34***	0.34***	0.34***	0.34***	0.31***
Urban	-0.10	-0.05	-0.06	-0.07	-0.12	-0.13
Rural	0.35*	0.38*	0.37*	0.41*	0.42*	0.46*
Catholic	-0.05	-0.09	-0.09	-0.01	-0.10	-0.09
NAIS	1.05	1.01	1.01	1.06	1.02	1.18

(continues)

TABLE 5.2 *(continued)*

Other private	-0.56	-0.59	-0.70*	-0.68*	-0.73*	-0.85*
Relative influence of tests in evaluating principal		-0.14	-0.13	-0.08	-0.09	-0.09
Principal's influence on hiring teachers		0.02	0.00	0.01	0.00	0.03
Principal's influence on setting teachers' performance standards		0.10	0.11	0.12	0.12	0.11
Test results sent to parents		0.14*	0.13*	0.13*	0.14*	0.12
Teacher's control over content			-0.03	-0.04	-0.06	-0.07
Teacher's control over teaching technique			0.19*	0.15	0.14	0.11
Relative importance of absolute achievement in grading			0.02	-0.02	0.02	0.07
Relative importance of individual improvement in grading			-0.25	-0.28*	-0.34**	-0.43**
Time spent instructing whole class				0.07	0.07	0.08
Time spent instructing small group				-0.04	-0.06	-0.05
Time spent instructing individuals				0.28**	0.26**	0.25**
Time spent maintaining order				-0.20**	-0.18*	-0.14*

(continues)

TABLE 5.2 *(continued)*

Teacher keeps records of who turned in assignments			0.14	0.15	0.11
Teacher returns assignments with grades and corrections			0.22*	0.20*	0.21*
Teacher discusses completed assignments in class			0.04	-0.01	-0.02
Emphasis on developing problem solving & inquiry skills				0.29**	0.26*
Emphasis on teaching scientific facts and principles				-0.16	-0.16
Emphasis on increasing students' interest in science				0.18	0.17
Emphasis on importance of science in everyday life				0.12	0.16
Emphasis on developing systematic observation skills				-0.04	-0.05
Emphasis on application of science in environmental issues				-0.04	-0.05
Student usually works hard for good grades					0.46**
Student often completes homework					0.20*
Student is often disruptive in class					-0.31***
Adjusted R^2	0.639	0.640	0.640	0.643	0.644	0.650

[a] based on 3390 cases for whom questionnaires are available from tenth grade science teachers; weighted by panel weight.
[b] * p<.05; ** p<.01; ***p<.001

autonomy. Each of these items is measured on a five-point scale, ranging from "no influence" to "major influence." Finally in Model B, we include a measure of how often standardized test results are provided to the parents or guardians of students in the school. With five response levels ranging from "never" to "always," this item reflects the degree to which there is substantive contact between the school and families which focuses on test scores and academic achievement.

In building our models, we suspected that part of the association between a school's reliance on external standards and a student's academic growth could be explained by particular classroom policies and practices. For example, to the extent that the relative influence of tests in evaluating the principal and sending test results to parents were significant predictors of learning, we wanted to determine whether some of this predictive power could be explained by patterns of teacher autonomy and classroom practices.

To accomplish this objective, Model C introduces variables measuring teachers' control over content coverage and teaching techniques, and teachers' grading practices. Teacher's control over selecting content, topics, and skills to be taught and their control over selecting instructional techniques are both measured on a six-point scale, ranging from "no control" to "complete control." We expected that in schools guided by external standards the curricular content would be determined outside the classroom and likely to be linked with standardized student achievement assessments. The other two variables added in Model C are the relative importance of absolute level of achievement in grading students and the relative importance of individual improvement or progress over past performance in grading students. These two variables indicate whether the teacher reports about using absolute level of achievement or individual improvement as measures for determining students' grades at least as much as he or she relies on each of five other criteria. The five other criteria are; a) achievement relative to the rest of the class, b) effort, c) class participation, d) completing homework assignments, and e) consistently attending class.

Having incorporated measures of the teacher's reliance on external standards, we wanted to see whether any effects on academic growth could be partially explained by particular teaching practices. Models D and E introduce several teaching practices. Model D focuses on the teachers' classroom management practices, such as the time spent instructing the whole class, time spent instructing small groups, time spent instructing individuals, and time spent maintaining order. Each of these is measured on a six-point scale, ranging from "none of class time" to "75-100 percent of class time." Model D also includes "teacher keeps record of who turned in assignments," "teacher returns assignments with grades or corrections," and "teacher discusses completed assignments in class." Each of these measures takes one of four levels, ranging from "never" to "all of the time."

Model E introduces items describing the teacher's focus on subject matter content. Mathematics teachers in the sample were asked how much emphasis they gave to each of twelve teaching objectives. Science teachers were asked about ten teaching objectives. Our mathematics model includes six of the items from the mathematics teachers' list. Our science model includes six items which are similar to the mathematics items in terms of their pedagogical functions but which were described in the questionnaire so as to be relevant to the teaching of science. The items are intended to represent a wide range of substantive areas of teaching while avoiding problems of extreme multicollinearity in the model estimation.[2] Each measure takes one of four levels, ranging from "no emphasis" to "heavy emphasis."

Finally, Model F incorporates measures of student behavior. We expect that students in output-driven schools and classrooms would exhibit more achievement-oriented behavior than students in schools that did not demonstrate output-driven characteristics. Such academic behavior should translate into higher achievement. Thus, Model F also includes teacher reports about whether the student usually works hard for good grades (1="yes"; 0="no" or "don't know"), how often the student completes homework assignments, and how often the student is disruptive in class (each on a five-point scale ranging from "never" to "all of the time"). We anticipated positive and significant coefficients for the first two of these measures, indicating that "better" behavior and effort is positively associated with academic growth. We anticipated a negative and significant coefficient for the third of these measures, indicating that disruptive behavior is negatively associated with academic growth. Further, because we hypothesized that students in output-driven schools and classrooms would exhibit achievement-oriented behavior, we anticipated that the significant effects of the measures of student behavior would attenuate the estimated direct effects of the various output measures at the school level and by the teacher in the classroom. We now turn to an examination of the empirical findings.

Results for Mathematics

In Table 5.1, Model A reflects first and foremost that much of the variation in tenth grade mathematics test scores can be explained by variation in eighth grade mathematics test scores. This baseline model explains over seventy-seven percent of the variance in tenth grade scores. Most of the explanatory power comes from the inclusion of the eighth grade score and the squared term. Additionally, Model A shows negative and significant coefficients for Hispanic and African American students, and positive and significant coefficients for students in Catholic schools and those with more educated parents.[3]

When the four measures of school-level organization and accountability are introduced in Model B, the coefficient for test results being sent to parents is positive and significant. This indicates that student achievement is higher when parents are kept apprised of test scores. The other three coefficients introduced in Model B are not significantly different from zero.

The results from Model C show the effects of teachers' control of content and technique, and grading practices. Some important points are suggested by the coefficients for these measures. The teacher's control over content is estimated to have a negative and significant effect, while the teacher's control over teaching technique has a positive and significant effect. Further, there is a positive and significant effect for the relative importance of absolute achievement in grading, while the effect of the relative importance of individual improvement is not significant.

Several other points can be made about Model C. First, introducing the measures of teacher control and grading practices does not markedly affect the estimates for the measures of school-level organization and accountability (except that the coefficient for principal's influence on setting teacher's performance standards does increase just enough in Model C to gain significance). Examining the stability of the school-level variables was one part of our investigation of whether effects of output-driven characteristics are mediated by specific policies and classroom practices. Although we do not find strong evidence of this sort of indirect effect as we examine Model C, the issue will be relevant again as we move to Models D, E, and F.

Second, in Model C the estimated effect for students in "other private" schools increases to the point of significance. Further exploratory analyses revealed that this change is specifically tied to the introduction of the measures of grading practices that appear to be more common in non-Catholic and non-NAIS private schools. When in place, these practices positively affect gains in mathematics achievement.

Model D introduces measures of the teacher's use of time and other classroom practices. There is a positive and significant effect for the teacher spending time instructing the whole class, while there is a negative and significant effect for the teacher spending time maintaining order and discipline. Further, the model shows a negative and significant effect for the teacher keeping records of who turned in assignments, while there is a positive and significant effect for the teacher discussing completed assignments in class.

With the introduction of these classroom practice items in Model D, it is noteworthy that the estimated effect for students in Catholic schools drops to insignificance, while the estimated effect for students in "other private" schools shows a further increase in magnitude and significance. Also, the estimated effects of the teacher's control over content and teaching technique drops from significance at the .05 level. However, teacher's control over content will be seen to regain significance in Models E and F. Teacher's control over teaching technique regains significance in Model E, but returns to insignificance in Model F. Again, these patterns inform our investigation of the effects of output-driven characteristics being mediated by classroom practices.

Model E adds the various items about curricular emphases in mathematics classes. Two of these items have significantly positive coefficients. These are an emphasis on understanding the nature of proof and an emphasis on the importance of mathematics in basic and applied sciences. Two other items have significantly negative effects. These are an emphasis on the importance of mathematics in everyday life and an emphasis on performing computations with speed and accuracy.

Finally, Model F introduces three measures of student behavior and effort. The model shows positive and significant coefficients for the measures of how hard the student usually works for good grades and how often the student completes homework. A negative and significant coefficient is seen for the measure of how often the student is disruptive in class. With the introduction of these three measures of student behavior and effort, the coefficient for male increases dramatically. This suggests that teachers report that males do not work as hard for good grades and complete their homework less often than females, and disrupt class more often. Once we have established controls for these detrimental aspects of behavior, however, males are characterized by significantly more growth in mathematics achievement than are females.

Results for Science

Model A reveals negative coefficients for all minority students (Asian American, Hispanic and African American students), a positive coefficient for students in rural schools, males, and parental education. The baseline model for science explains about 64 percent of the variance in tenth grade science test scores, which is slightly lower than the variance explained in the mathematics model.

In Model B we see a positive and significant coefficient for test results being sent to parents, which is similar to what was seen in the mathematics models. The other coefficients introduced in Model B are not statistically significant.

Model C reveals a positive and significant coefficient for the teacher's control over teaching technique, which again mirrors what was seen in the mathematics models. In contrast to what was seen for mathematics, however, Model C for science achievement does not reveal significant coefficients for the teacher's control over content or the relative importance of absolute achievement in grading. The coefficient for the relative importance of individual improvement in grading, though, is negative and near significance in Model C. In the subsequent Models D, E, and F, this coefficient does become negative and significant.

Model D displays a positive effect for the teacher spending time instructing individuals, while there is a negative effect for the teacher spending time maintaining order and discipline. Further, the model shows a positive effect for the teacher returning homework assignments with grades and corrections. With the introduction of these classroom practice items in Model D, the coefficient for the relative importance of individual improvement becomes significantly negative at the .05 level, while the estimated effect for the teacher's control over teaching technique is reduced to non-significance.

In Model E, when the teaching focuses are introduced, emphasis on developing problem solving and inquiring skills is shown to have a significantly positive effect. Finally, in Model F, when students' behavioral measures are added, it is found that "student usually works hard for good grades" and "student often completes homework" have significantly positive effects, while "student is often disruptive in class" has a negative effect. The coefficients of the previous variables are stable, except for the coefficient for "test results sent to parents," which is reduced to non-significance in this final model.

Evidence of the Importance of Output-Driven Factors

Schools vary in the degree to which they rely on external standards. Based on the data, no school could be considered purely output-driven as described in Chapter 2. However, enough schools have a measure of reliance on external standards and some of the accompanying output-driven organizational characteristics such that we could explore the potential impact on student achievement of these practices. What we have found are positive and significant effects for some measures of reliance on external standards and actions that make schools publicly accountable. Further, these effects are partially mediated by how power and control is distributed in schools, and how teachers and students use their classroom time.

The direct effects of sending test scores home to parents indicate the importance of informing a family of its child's performance. Often times school systems will only release summary reports of district-wide achievement results by grade. These summary reports, while perhaps helpful for assessing average performance differences between districts, tend to obfuscate individual performance and can lull parents into believing that their child is scoring at or above average. With information on their own child's performance, parents can learn how their child's scores compare to other students in the school or district, as well as learn how their child is progressing from year to year. Knowing that their child is scoring below average may activate parents to place pressure on the school to implement measures to enhance performance, as well as engage in some at-home activities such as one-on-one tutoring.

The strong direct effects on mathematics achievement of external control of curricular content and the use of absolute measures of achievement in grading emphasize the importance of removing discretionary action over what gets taught and how it should be evaluated. It appears to be beneficial to students to limit the control teachers have over curricular content while granting control to teachers in determining teaching techniques. By placing control of the content outside of the teacher's discretion, it lessens the chance that key curricular topics will not be covered and enhances the probability that topics will be taught sequentially from year to year.

It may be that such practices are easier to institute with respect to mathematics than science because of the hierarchical structure of the mathematics curriculum. The diffuseness of the science curricular structure may make gains in performance more difficult to link to school organizational factors, since for many students the knowledge gained from one year of science work to another may not necessarily be cumulative. In addition, the diffuse science curriculum often mean that test items are not related to a particular students' science courses. For example, one student may take earth science as a freshman and biology as a sophomore, while another takes biology first and then earth science. Both of these students may perform poorly on the chemistry section of an external examination.[4]

The importance of setting clear standards is also seen in the relationship between teachers and students. When the teacher emphasizes clear standards for achievement in his or her grading practices, students achieve at higher levels. This effect remains consistently positive regardless of the teacher's instructional technique or content covered in the course. It should also be noted that placing an emphasis on "improvement," while intended to encourage academically struggling students to work harder, does not appear to increase student achievement. If anything, the consistently negative coefficient (significant for science but not for mathematics) suggests that grading on the basis of improvement may depress students' achievement. This illustrates the importance of clear standards in the output-driven model as a means to focus students on what they need to know and giving their teachers the freedom to help them gain that knowledge.

The enhancement of student growth, it seems, flows both directly from a system of public accountability and external controls, and indirectly through teachers' practices. Along these indirect paths, the existence of an output-driven school and classroom seems to encourage or facilitate particular teacher practices. It is largely through these teacher practices, in turn, that students benefit in terms of their academic growth. To support these claims, we traced the estimated effects of the teacher's control over teaching technique and the relative importance of absolute achievement in grading across the models of mathematics achievement. The direct effect of the relative importance of absolute achievement in grading steadily decreased (but retained some positive significance) with the introduction of teacher practices, curricular emphases, and student behavior and effort. Many of the measures of particular teacher practices, emphases, behavior, and effort, in turn, had positive effects. Taken together, these findings suggest both direct and indirect effects of the external standards.

Our findings also show the importance of coupling external standards with teachers' control over instructional techniques. With the introduction of particular teaching practices in the mathematics models, the direct effect of teacher's control over technique dropped to non-significance. With the introduction of specific curricular emphases, the direct effect of teacher's control over teaching technique returned to significance. A plausible explanation for this pattern is that controlling for the use of certain overarching teaching styles (e.g., whole-class instruction as opposed to small group instruction), and for curricular emphases, there is an added benefit to students when teachers retain considerable control over teaching techniques. The benefit may result from the freedom teachers have to fine-tune their styles and customize the classroom environment to fit their particular students.

What happens when teachers are allowed to fine-tune their styles and customize their classroom environments? With the introduction of measures of student behavior and effort in the final models, the direct effect of teacher's control over teaching techniques decreased to the point of insignificance. The measures of student behavior and effort, however, had significant effects in the expected directions. These patterns suggest that teachers are able to use their control over teaching techniques to inspire students to work hard and behave well. Hard work and good behavior, in turn, appear to translate into positive academic growth.

Finally, we return to the estimated effects of particular curricular emphases. Emphasizing an understanding of the nature of proof and developing an awareness of the importance of mathematics in the basic and applied sciences are positively associated with student growth in mathematics. Emphasizing an awareness of the importance of mathematics in everyday life and emphasizing computations performed with speed and accuracy are negatively associated with student growth. In general it can be said that, in these models and other investigations we did of the twelve items regarding teachers' curricular objectives in mathematics, an emphasis on fairly traditional fact-based and logic-based instruction appears to be beneficial to student growth. On the other hand, an emphasis on liking mathematics and linking mathematics to everyday life and business and industry does not appear to benefit students' academic growth.

We find slightly different output-driven effects for science than math, which are not unexpected. First, mathematics is more hierarchically and sequentially organized than science (Stevenson, Schiller and Schneider 1994), so gains in test scores can be more directly traced to curricular content.[5] Second, mathematics learning is more strongly tied to in-school instruction than other subjects. Thus, we did not expect to find as clear connections between science achievement gains and school and teacher output-driven factors as we had with math.[6]

Although there are fewer direct effects in the science models, we continue to find that gains in science achievement are negatively associated with ambiguous grading measures such as individual improvement. The indirect effects continue to demonstrate, as with mathematics models, that teacher techniques that motivate students to work hard for grades, complete their homework and behave in classrooms are positively associated with academic growth.

The positive results for the output-driven measures in the mathematics and science models point to the importance of external standards, public accountability, and uncompromising assessment of student performance for enhancing gains in academic achievement. With external requirements, administrators, teachers, and students are more aware of what is expected of them. Rewarding students on the basis of clear expectations can be a motivating force that has strong effects on academic performance.

Notes

1. The squared term is included to account for the curvilinearity seen when tenth grade test scores are plotted against eighth grade test scores. Some ceiling effects are apparent from such plots and must be accounted for in our models.

2. A principal component analysis was performed using the twelve mathematics teaching objective items. Three principal components were retained as an adequate summary of the data. Each of these three components had especially large loadings (large in absolute value) for two of the teaching objective items. These six items (two from each of the three principal components) were retained in our analyses. These six retained items are listed in Table 5.1. Six of the ten science teaching objective items were selected, based on their conceptual similarity to the mathematics items. These six items are listed in Table 5.2.

3. We were concerned about the samples and the generalizability of our results because of missing data on some teacher and classroom measures. To examine these issues, we first compared univariate distributions for our independent variables for the NELS:88-94 first follow-up longitudinal panel with distributions for our final mathematics and science samples (i.e., the samples reflected in Tables 5.1 and 5.2). The distributions were quite comparable.

Further, we estimated Model A for mathematics and science, using all non-missing cases in the longitudinal panel. The numbers of cases were 15,014 for mathematics and 14,903 for science. Thus, relatively few of the 17,424 cases in the nationally representative panel were lost in these "exploratory" estimations. The exploratory estimations of Model A suggested that the somewhat surprising coefficients for Asian Americans in Tables 5.1 and 5.2 are not due to the selection of our samples. Specifically, the coefficient for Asian Americans in the exploratory science model is negative and significant. This matches the negative and significant coefficient in Model A of Table 5.2. The coefficient for Asian Americans in the exploratory mathematics model is positive and significant, which compares with the non-significant coefficient in Model A of Table 5.1.

Finally, we examined Models A through C, based on the cases with non-missing values for the variables of Model C. Again, these estimations provided somewhat larger samples than the samples of Tables 5.1 and 5.2. The results, shown in Appendix Tables 5.A.1 and 5.A.2, are quite similar to the results in Tables 5.1 and 5.2.

4. Table 5.A.3 shows the linkages between NELS:88-94 base year and first follow-up test items and specific science subjects.

5. In another analysis we investigated the topics covered in the NELS:88-94 science tests across the various waves. We found that certain topics such as chemistry were covered unevenly. (See Appendix Table 5.A.3 for a comparison of the eighth and tenth grade tests.) We expect that gains in science therefore reflect course-taking behaviors to a large extent. For example, a student might have scored well on the eighth grade test due to a strong chemistry background, continued learning a lot about chemistry but relatively little about physics and, consequently, scored relatively poorly on the tenth grade test. Such a student would show relatively little growth due to her/his particular sequence of courses. This meager

growth obscures the fact that the student has, in fact, continued to gain new knowledge in some areas of science.

6. We also estimated our models for achievement gains in history and English. For history we find that the effect of test results sent home to parents is positive and significant, as is the effect of relative importance of absolute achievement in grading. For English, the effect of relative influence of tests in evaluating the principals is positive and significant, as is the effect of the principal's influence on setting teacher's performance standards.

TABLE 5.A.1 OLS Coefficients for Models of Tenth Grade Mathematics Achievement: With Larger Sample Than That Used in Estimations of Table 5.1[a,b]

Intercept	-5.17***	-5.90***	-8.53***
Eighth grade math test	1.63***	1.63***	1.62***
(Eighth grade math test)^2	-0.01***	-0.01***	-0.01***
Asian American	-0.69	-0.73	-0.75
Hispanic	-1.04**	-1.12**	-1.07**
African American	-2.47***	-2.61***	-2.49***
Male	-0.18	-0.15	-0.12
Parents' education	0.84***	0.83***	0.81***
Urban	0.14	0.02	0.00
Rural	-0.30	-0.31	-0.24
Catholic	1.06**	1.19**	1.19**
NAIS	0.40	0.69	0.53
Other private	1.15	1.23	1.34*

(continues)

TABLE 5.A.1 *(continued)*

Relative influence of tests in evaluating principal		0.40	0.39
Principal's influence on hiring teachers		-0.35**	-0.36**
Principal's influence on setting teachers' performance standards		0.25*	0.27*
Test results sent to parents		0.27**	0.23*
Teacher's control over content			-0.13*
Teacher's control over teaching technique			0.58***
Relative importance of absolute achievement in grading			0.73***
Relative importance of individual improvement in grading			-0.15
Adjusted R²	0.772	0.773	0.775

[a] based on 4954 cases for whom questionnaires are available from tenth grade mathematics teachers; weighted by panel weight.
[b] * p<.05; ** p<.01; ***p<.001

TABLE 5.A.2 OLS Coefficients for Models of Tenth Grade Science Achievement: With Larger Sample Than That Used in Estimations of Table 5.2[a,b]

Variables	Model A	Model B	Model C
Intercept	2.15**	1.24	0.57
Eighth grade science test	0.69***	0.68***	0.69***
(Eighth grade science test)^2	-0.004*	-0.004*	-0.004*
Eighth grade math test	0.19***	0.19***	0.18***
Asian American	-0.85**	-0.85**	-0.87**
Hispanic	-0.64**	-0.62**	-0.62**
African American	-1.42***	-1.38***	-1.35***
Male	1.07***	1.07***	1.09***
Parents' education	0.36***	0.36***	0.36***
Urban	-0.16	-0.12	-0.12
Rural	0.35*	0.36*	0.35*
Catholic	-0.13	-0.14	-0.18
NAIS	0.79	0.74	0.70

(continues)

TABLE 5.A.2 *(continued)*

Other private	-0.59	-0.62	-0.78*
Relative influence of tests in evaluating principal		-0.28*	-0.27*
Principal's influence on hiring teachers		-0.04	-0.06
Principal's influence on setting teachers' performance standards		0.13*	0.12*
Test results sent to parents		0.15**	0.15**
Teacher's control over content			0.04
Teacher's control over teaching technique			0.11
Relative importance of absolute achievement in grading			0.02
Relative importance of individual improvement in grading			-0.27*
Adjusted R^2	0.635	0.636	0.636

[a] based on 4104 cases for whom questionnaires are available from tenth grade science teachers; weighted by panel weight. [b] * p<.05; ** p<.01; ***p<.001

TABLE 5.A.3 Subject Area of Science Test Items: NELS:88-94 Base Year (1988) and First Follow-Up (1990)

Key Words of Item	Item in Test		Subject Area			
	1988	1990	Chemistry	Physics	Biology	Other
Evidence	✓					×
Solar system	✓					×
Solubility	✓	✓	×			
Experimental design	✓	✓				×
Sun and moon	✓	✓		×		
Simple reflex	✓	✓			×	
Astronauts and sound	✓			×		
Eclipse	✓			×		
Oxygen in sea	✓				×	
States of matter	✓	✓	×			
Ocean water	✓		×			
Earth around sun	✓	✓		×		
Fish and oxygen	✓				×	
Mixing	✓	✓	×			
Respiration	✓	✓			×	
Reading graph	✓	✓			×	

(continues)

TABLE 5.A.3 *(continued)*

Key Words of Item	Item in Test		Subject Area			
	1988	1990	Chemistry	Physics	Biology	Other
Marine algae	✓	✓			×	
Signs of storm	✓	✓				×
Chemical change	✓	✓	×			
Liquid and solids	✓	✓	×			
Air currents	✓	✓				×
Food chain	✓	✓			×	
$C_3H_8 + 5O_2 \to$	✓	✓	×			
Model and observation	✓	✓				×
Guinea pigs, genes	✓	✓			×	
Density of granite		✓		×		
Board balance		✓		×		
Contour map		✓		×		
Light and lens		✓		×		
Radioisotope half-life		✓		×		
Curve and equilibrium		✓				×
Electrical circuit		✓		×		

Appendix 5.1

Variable Construction and Univariate Statistics[a]

Dependent Variables

Tenth grade math test
F12XMIRR, Mathematics IRT-estimated number right in 1990. Mean = 45.24; s.d. = 13.56; range (16.65, 72.76).

Tenth grade science test
F12XSIRR, Science IRT-estimated number right in 1990. Mean = 22.02; s.d. = 5.95; range (10.09, 34.68).

Independent Variables

Eighth grade math test
 BY2XMIRR, Mathematics IRT-estimated number right in 1988. Mean = 37.54; s.d. = 11.66; range (16.38, 66.81).

Eighth grade science test
 BY2XSIRR, Science IRT-estimated number right in 1988. Mean = 19.22; s.d. = 4.80; range (9.49, 32.88).

Asian American, Hispanic, African American
 Dummy variables constructed from F1RACE, with *white* as the excluded reference category. Proportions = 0.04, 0.07, and 0.09, respectively.

Male
 Dummy variable constructed from F1SEX, with *Female* as the excluded reference category. Proportion = 0.50.

Parents' education
 Six-point scale constructed from F1PARED. Mean = 3.16; s.d. = 1.17; range (1,6).

---

[a] All univariate statistics are for the sample used in the mathematics models of Table 5.1 (n=4315) except for the statistics for the two measures of science achievement and the six measures of science curricular emphasis, which are for the sample used in the science models of Table 5.2 (n=3390).

Urban, Rural
Dummy variables constructed from G10URBAN, with *Suburban* as the excluded reference category. Proportions = 0.07, 0.01, and 0.02, respectively.

Catholic, NAIS, Other private
Dummy variables constructed from G10CTRL2, with *Public* as the excluded reference category.

Relative influence of tests in evaluating principal
Dummy variable for "strong relative influence" constructed from F1C103A through F1C103D, with "weak relative influence" as the excluded reference category. Proportion = 0.27.

Principal's influence on hiring teachers
Five-point scale constructed from F1C98A. Mean = 4.63; s.d. = 0.73; range (1,5).

Principal's influence on setting teachers' performance standards
Five-point scale constructed from F1C98D. Mean = 4.24; s.d. = 0.84.

Test results sent to parents
Six-point scale, constructed from F1C64. Mean = 4.44; s.d. = 0.71; range (0,5).

Teacher's control over content
Six-point scale constructed from F1T2_17B. Mean = 4.23; s.d. = 0.53; range (1,6).

Teacher's control over teaching technique
Six-point scale constructed from F1T2_17C. Mean = 5.57; s.d. = 0.57; range (1,6).

Relative importance of absolute achievement in grading
Dummy variable for "strong relative importance" constructed from F1T3_24A, B, D, E, F, and G, with "weak relative importance" as the excluded reference category. Proportion = 0.54.

Relative importance of individual improvement in grading
Dummy variable for "strong relative importance" constructed from F1T3_24C, B, D, E, F, and G, with "weak relative importance" as the excluded reference category. Proportion = 0.36.

Time spent instructing whole class
Six-point scale constructed from F1T2_16A. Mean = 4.66; s.d. = 0.90; range (1,6).

Time spent instructing small group
Six-point scale constructed from F1T2_16B. Mean = 2.34; s.d. = 0.89; range (1,6).

Time spent instructing individuals
Six-point scale constructed from F1T2_16C. Mean = 2.82; s.d. = 0.85; range (1,6).

Time spent maintaining order
Six-point scale constructed from F1T2_16D. Mean = 2.01; s.d. = 0.90; range (1,6).

Teacher keeps records of who turned in assignments
Four-point scale constructed from F1T2_10A. Mean = -1.59; s.d. = 0.81; range (-4,-1).

Teacher returns assignments with grades and corrections
Four-point scale constructed from F1T2_10B. Mean = -2.26; s.d. = 1.08; range (-4,-1).

Teacher discusses completed assignments in class
Four-point scale constructed from F1T2_10C. Mean = -1.34; s.d. = 0.63; range (-4,-1).

Emphasis on understanding the nature of proof
Four-point scale constructed from F1T2M19B. Mean = 2.63; s.d. = 1.01; range (1,4).

Emphasis on memorizing facts, rules, and steps
Four-point scale constructed from F1T2M19C. Mean = 3.03; s.d. = 0.73; range (1,4).

Emphasis on becoming interested in mathematics
Four-point scale constructed from F1T2M19D. Mean = 3.15; s.d. = 0.72; range (1,4).

Emphasis on importance of mathematics in everyday life
Four-point scale constructed from F1T2M19F. Mean = 3.22; s.d. = 0.73; range (1,4).

Emphasis on performing computations with speed and accuracy
Four-point scale constructed from F1T2M19H. Mean = 2.97; s.d. = 0.77; range (1,4).

Emphasis on importance of math in basic and applied sciences
Four-point scale constructed from F1T2M19I. Mean = 2.87; s.d. = 0.79; range (1,4).

Emphasis on developing problem solving and inquiry skills
Four-point scale constructed from F1T2S19E. Mean = 3.29; s.d. = 0.71; range (1,4).

Emphasis on teaching scientific facts and principals
Four-point scale constructed from F1T2S19B. Mean = 3.64; s.d. = 0.53; range (1,4).

Emphasis on increasing students' interest in science
Four-point scale constructed from F1T2S19A. Mean = 3.46; s.d. = 0.57; range (1,4).

Emphasis on importance of science in everyday life
Four-point scale constructed from F1T2S19G. Mean = 3.49; s.d. = 0.61; range (1,4).

Emphasis on developing systematic observation skills

Four-point scale constructed from F1T2S19H. Mean = 3.15; s.d. = 0.73; range (1,4).

Emphasis on application of science in environmental issues
Four-point scale constructed from F1T2S19I. Mean = 3.17; s.d. = 0.72; range (1,4).

Student usually works hard for good grades
Dummy variable constructed from F1T1_2, with *No* as the excluded reference category. Proportion = 0.66.

Student often completes homework
Five-point scale constructed from F1T1_15. Mean = 3.93; s.d. = 0.95; range (1,5).

Student is often disruptive in class
Five-point scale constructed from F1T1_20. Mean = 1.64; s.d. = 0.84; range (1,5).

6

External Examinations as an Incentive System

Kathryn S. Schiller

Theories concerning output-driven systems suggest that lack of a strong external evaluation system is a major problem in the American educational system. Setting standards internally to the school or to the classroom allows for the negotiation of evaluation criteria, such as students' good behavior, rather than achievement, to be the basis for teachers awarding good grades. An important feature of output-driven systems is the development of external standards and evaluations (Chapter 2). In classrooms, this means that the teacher does not set the standards for awarding grades or other forms of evaluation. Instead, the teacher takes on the role of coach to help students to develop the skills and knowledge needed to meet the externally determined standards. Thus, external evaluations are a key to establishing an incentive system that encourages high performance, as teachers and students work toward a common goal of high achievement.

American high schools do not entirely lack an external evaluation system. College entrance examinations, the most widely used of which is the Scholastic Aptitude Test (SAT), can be considered an externally derived system for evaluating high school graduates. While the usefulness and fairness of these examinations is often questioned, a large percentage of American universities and colleges use these examinations when evaluating prospective students in the college admission process (Crouse and Trusheim 1988, 1991; Crouse 1985; Hanford 1985; Slack and Porter 1980). Thus, how well students perform on these tests has considerable influence on which type of school, if any, will admit them.

The goal of this chapter is not to defend or attack the college entrance examinations used in the U.S. Instead, the SAT is used as an example of an external evaluation that may affect student achievement. The analyses in this chapter explore the effect of planning to take the SAT on students' growth in mathematics achievement over the last two years of high school.

Specifically, we look for evidence that this examination provides incentives for students to increase their academic achievement. This is done by showing that plans to take the SAT are related to higher growth in mathematics achievement, independent of the students' educational aspirations, social backgrounds, and success in school. Additionally, this relationship is strongest for those students whose grades are borderline for college admission or who are educationally and socially disadvantaged. These are groups for whom college attendance is frequently problematic, due to a lack of social or financial resources, or due to questionable academic records. Both of these potential obstacles to college attendance might be overcome, or at least lowered, by a student performing well on the SAT. Thus, the SAT may provide a greater incentive for achievement for these students, in comparison to those who have more resources or excellent academic records.

The SAT as an External Examination System

The SAT is administered by the Educational Testing Service (ETS), which was founded in 1947 with the help of the College Entrance Examination Board (often referred to as the College Board). This board has a membership of over 2,500 colleges, schools, and educational associations. The examination was designed to assess the quality of high school graduates and their potential to succeed in postsecondary education. An outgrowth of intelligence testing, the SAT was initially touted as an examination which allowed all students to compete on a level playing field, regardless of which high school they attend (for a review of the history of the SAT, see Crouse and Trusheim 1988).

Currently, many colleges and universities use performance on the SAT as one of the main predictors of students' readiness for a postsecondary curriculum. Crouse and Trusheim (1991) report that at least 1,600 out of 3,500 four-year colleges and universities in the U.S. use the SAT as part of their admissions process. SAT scores are often used for more than just admissions decisions. Many competitive scholarships are at least partially based on applicants' SAT scores, thereby affecting students' college financing opportunities. SAT scores may also affect what a student is able to study, since some highly competitive academic programs require certain cutoff scores for admission (Wainer and Steinberg 1992; Pallas and Alexander 1983). In addition, students' SAT scores may determine whether they can play college sports, since the National Collegiate Athletic Association requires freshmen playing varsity sports to have a minimum score on the SAT or another college entrance examination (NCES 1995).

As the percentage of high school graduates attending college has increased, so has the number of students taking the SAT. Between 1980 and 1990, the percentage of high school sophomores planning to continue their education past high school rose from 73.5% to 89.1% (Schiller 1994; Rasinski et al. 1993). Most of this increase was in students planning to obtain at least a bachelor's degree from a four-year college or university. This increase in educational aspirations also meant an increase in the percentage of students taking the SAT. During the same decade, the percentage of seniors who took the SAT increased from 36.6% in 1982 (NCES 1987) to 46.5% in 1992 (NCES 1994). The importance of the examination is also reflected in the involvement of parents and schools in helping students prepare for the examinations, with most schools providing special courses to coach students for the SAT and the vast majority of parents encouraging their children to study for it.

In 1987, about 1.5 million high school juniors and seniors took the SAT, many of them for the second or third time. Almost 80% of students taking the SAT believe that their scores should have a "great deal" or "a fair amount" of influence on college admissions officers' decisions (Crouse 1985). Only 30% of students, however, reported that they expected their SAT scores to be one of their strong points for getting into college. At the same time, close to 20% of test takers reported being "very nervous" and about 56% "a little nervous" about taking the SAT.

> No one takes the SAT for fun. The test is three hours of nail-biting anxiety for many high school students. They take the test because they plan to apply to one of the more than 1,500 colleges that require or strongly recommend it for admissions. (Crouse and Trusheim 1988: p. 4)

It should be noted, however, that performance on the SAT or another college entrance examination is not the only major factor influencing students' opportunities for postsecondary education. Admissions personnel also use other criteria such as high school grades, participation in extracurricular activities, and letters of recommendation when evaluating applicants. Some schools do not even require SAT or other college admission test scores, making it possible for high school graduates to attend a college or university without taking a college entrance examination.

In fact, some colleges and universities use high school grades as the sole indicator of probable success in postsecondary schooling. Critics of the SAT argue that high school grades are as good an indicator as test scores, or possibly even better, of postsecondary success (Keller, Crouse and Trusheim 1994; Crouse and Trusheim 1988, 1991; Crouse 1985; Jencks and

Crouse 1982; Slack and Porter 1980). They argue that the number of "incorrect admissions," which are students who are admitted or rejected when they should not have been, is not substantively reduced by using a combination of SAT scores and high school grades to predict college freshman grades, a commonly used indicator of success in college. Using an expected freshman grade point average (GPA) of 2.5 (C+) as the cutoff point for admission, Crouse (1985) estimates that only 9.2% of colleges' admissions decisions would be different if SAT scores plus high school class rank, instead of rank alone, were used to predict freshman grades. Thus, critics argue, SAT scores are redundant in relation to high school grades as a tool for evaluating admissions applications.

Supporters of the SAT counter Crouse and his colleagues' argument about the redundancy of SAT scores by noting that the sample they use is limited to only students who took the SAT *and* who attended college, thereby eliminating those students who did not take the SAT or did not attend college. The analyses in this chapter differ from their research, and most of the other research concerning the SAT, in that students are included regardless of whether or not they took the SAT and regardless of their plans for postsecondary schooling. This means that the borderline students, those most likely to be subject to "incorrect admissions" decisions, are included in these analyses. SAT scores may be most crucial for these students' educational futures.

This chapter also focuses on the SAT as an institutional feature of the American educational system and its possible influences on student achievement. Proponents of the SAT argue that the examination is part of a system of "checks and balances" in which the accuracy of grades as a measure of students' developed abilities should be confirmed by test scores administered independently from the school (Hanford 1985; Jackson 1980). The logic of this argument is that the test is highly reliable and comparable from student to student across schools. Unlike the SAT, GPA often measures distributions of achievement within schools rather than between them. Supporters argue, and a few opponents agree, that the elimination of external evaluations may have undesirable effects, including grade inflation and watered down curriculum (Hanford 1985; Crouse and Trusheim 1988, 1991; Crouse 1985). For example, schools or teachers may ease grading standards to increase the likelihood of their students getting into good schools. Or, students may feel greater pressure to take easier courses to get better grades.

As the system works now, the courses students take in high school clearly affect how well they perform on the SAT. Initially, ETS and the College Board maintained that students' performance on the SAT should not reflect variations in high school courses. Since the 1980s, the examination's administrators have presented SAT scores as "indicators of developed abilities that are important to success in a wide range of academic programs" (Hanford 1985; Jackson 1980). They add that one of the most effective ways to develop those abilities is by taking academically challenging courses. One reason for this change in perspective was results from studies in the 1980s and 1990s that showed clear relationships between the curriculum students cover in high school courses and how well they do on the SAT (Gibbins and Bickel 1991; Becker 1990; Brody and Benbow 1990; Cooper 1987; Pallas and Alexander 1983). For example, Cooper (1987) and Brody and Benbow (1990) found a positive effect of taking foreign language courses on students' verbal SAT scores. They suggest that the verbal abilities measured by the SAT are really part and parcel of the repertoire of learning strategies that successful language learners hone through consistent practice, such as developing a sensitivity for nuance in the meaning of words and using contextual cues to guess the meaning of unknown words in a passage.

The mathematics section of the SAT is even more directly tied to the high school curriculum than is the verbal section. In its description of the examination, ETS states that the mathematics section of the SAT requires students to have knowledge of basic algebra and some intuitive notions of geometry (Jackson 1980). Research has confirmed this by clearly showing that students who have had more exposure to advanced mathematics have an advantage over those students who have not taken as many of those courses (Brody and Benbow 1990; Pallas and Alexander 1983). That advantage may come from training in abstract reasoning and problem solving, along with extensive practice computing. Pallas and Alexander (1983) find that 60% of the difference between boys and girls on the quantitative portion of the SAT can be attributed to course taking differences.

In summary, while students' performance on the SAT does not dictate their futures, those who perform poorly may find many doors to higher education closed to them. For example, Pallas and Alexander (1983) suggest that "low performance in mathematics [section of the SAT] may block entrance into select colleges and deter women from pursuing science and quantitative studies majors in college" (p. 170). The importance of the SAT to their futures may explain students' nervousness and anxiety about taking the SAT, which may translate into incentives for them to work harder in mathematics in order to achieve higher scores.

The Methods and Variables

Analyses

The analyses in this chapter explore how the SAT can act as an incentive system by determining whether sophomores who planned to take the examination had higher growth rates in mathematics over the last two years of high school compared to sophomores who did not have these plans. The analyses are divided into three parts. First, we describe the wide variety of sophomores from differing social backgrounds, curricular preparation, and educational aspirations who plan to take the SAT. Second, we determine the relationship between growth in mathematics achievement and sophomores' plans to take the SAT, taking into account students' social backgrounds, curricular preparation, and educational aspirations. These are factors that may potentially create a spurious relationship between students' plans to take the SAT and higher mathematics achievement. Third, we explore whether the relationship between mathematics growth and plans to take the SAT varies among students who differ in their educational aspirations, social backgrounds, and exposure to and success in mathematics. These variations are then used to suggest how the SAT may act as an incentive system for some high school students.

Sample

Throughout the analyses, sophomores who planned to take the SAT are compared to those who did not have such plans. The sample is drawn from the Second Follow-Up Panel of NELS:88-94, which consists of students who participated in all three data collections.[1] These analyses use those sophomores who answered the First Follow-Up question about whether they were planning to take the SAT (see Appendix Table 6.A.1 for a description of the variables used in this chapter and their sources).[2] Those who answered "I haven't thought about taking" or "No, I don't plan to take" the SAT are considered to be *not* planning to take the SAT. These students are grouped together, because an individual must be aware of the SAT and be planning to take it in order for the examination to act as an incentive for achievement.

The other group of sophomores consists of those planning to take the SAT, regardless of when they planned to do so. Of those sophomores planning to take the examination, the majority (57%) planned to do so as juniors and another 35% as seniors. The remaining 7% planned to take the SAT for the first time during the year they were sophomores. For the purposes of these analyses, all students who were planning to take the

TABLE 6.1 Sophomores' Plans to Take the SAT and Their Follow-Through on Those Plans

Sophomore Plans to Take the SAT	All Students	Takes the SAT	
		Yes	No
Yes	65.7%	59.7%	40.3%
No	34.3%	24.4%	75.6%

SAT, regardless of the year, are contrasted with those who had no such plans.

It should be stressed here that planning to take the SAT is different than actually doing so. A substantial proportion of sophomores change their minds by the time they graduate. The first column of Table 6.1 shows that a large majority of American sophomores (almost two-thirds) plan to take the SAT. The next two columns show how likely sophomores are to follow through on those plans. Almost 60% of those planning to take the SAT had taken it by the time they graduated. Conversely, almost a quarter of the sophomores who said they did *not* plan to take the SAT had apparently changed their minds by *taking* it before they graduated. This inconsistency of students' plans to take and actually taking the SAT suggests that studies which only include the latter may be missing important sections of the population: students who planned to take the SAT but did not, and those who never planned to take the examination.

Dependent Variable

Mathematics achievement, as measured on NELS:88-94 First and Second Follow-Ups, is the focus of the regression analysis because it is more sensitive to curriculum and school effects than are the other subject matter tests.[3] The dependent variable in the regression models is the senior mathematics test score (based on IRT measures). All the models include sophomore mathematics test score as a control for students' prior achievement. The square of the sophomore mathematics test score is also included in the models to control for a modest ceiling effect in the data (indicated by the statistically significant negative coefficients in the regression equations). By controlling on sophomore test score, regression coefficients for the other independent variables can be interpreted as

FIGURE 6.1: Percentage of Sophomores Planning to Take the SAT by Students' Educational Aspirations and Parents' Education

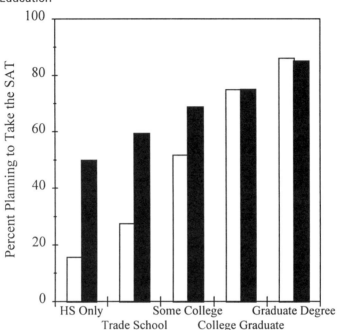

Students' Educational Expectations

Parents' Education

differences in mathematics achievement growth over the last two years of high school.[4] The metric is the number of correct answers gained on the senior test over the sophomore test score.

Control Variables

Three types of control variables are used in this chapter: social background, exposure to and success in mathematics, and educational aspirations. These three factors need to be taken into account because they may affect not only mathematics achievement and students' plans to take the SAT, but also, the relationship between mathematics achievement and students' plans to take the SAT. The latter is explored in the third set of analyses in this chapter.

Four variables are used as indicators of students' social backgrounds: gender, race/ethnicity, parents' education, and family income. Indicators for four racial or ethnic groups were created: African American, Asian American, Hispanic and white.[5] Parents' education and family income are used separately here, rather than as a composite for socioeconomic status, because they are expected to differently affect students' college aspirations. These four variables are used for two reasons: (1) they are the traditional social background variables used as controls in analyses of student achievement; and (2) they are related to both student achievement and plans to take the SAT (see the first set of analyses).

Exposure to and success in mathematics are measured by students' reports of the courses they took and the average grades they received as freshmen and sophomores. Mathematics courses taken by high school freshmen and sophomores are used in these analyses as a measure of the types of mathematics students have been exposed to at the time their plans to take the SAT are measured. Stevenson, Schiller and Schneider (1994) show that, given the hierarchical nature of the mathematics curriculum in high schools, students' courses are a measure of their location in a sequence of opportunities for learning. As with that earlier study, in these analyses students are divided into three groups: (1) students who took only Algebra I or General Mathematics; (2) those who took *either* Algebra II *or* Geometry; and (3) those who took *both* Algebra II *and* Geometry, *or* took some other advanced mathematics course. These classifications are particularly applicable to this study, because students' positions in a mathematics curriculum sequence are an important indicator of how prepared they are to take the SAT. As noted earlier, the mathematics section of the SAT focuses on problem solving skills that require a good working knowledge of high school algebra and geometry. Students who have taken *neither* Algebra II *nor* Geometry (group 1 above) as sophomores have not had the opportunity to master the skills ETS states are needed to do well on the SAT. Sophomores further along in the mathematics sequence have already covered at least some of the material included in the SAT and are on track to cover the rest before they need to take the examination.

Students' success in mathematics courses is another important dimension of their academic experiences, especially as it relates to their likelihood of being accepted by colleges. In these analyses, students' reports of their average mathematics grades as freshmen and sophomores are used as a measure of their success in mathematics. Although students tend to inflate their grades in self-reports, this is not a problem for these analyses, since these self-reports reflect students' perceptions of how well they are doing in mathematics. Those reporting higher grades may have confidence that their academic record will enhance their college applications, while those with lower grades may hope that higher SAT scores will offset a questionable academic record.

Because the main reason for taking the SAT is to get into college, sophomores' educational expectations are taken into account throughout these analyses. Sophomores were asked "how far in school do you think you will get?" with possible answers ranging from "less than high school" to "Ph.D., M.D., or other advanced professional degree." All sophomores, regardless of whether or not they think they will attend college, are included in these analyses for several reasons. As shown in the next section, even some sophomores who do not think they will attend college still report they are planning to take the SAT. Many of these sophomores may be keeping their options open,[6] or considering another type of postsecondary schooling, such as a competitive trade or vocational program, for which SAT scores are suggested or required.

Who Plans to Take College Entrance Examinations

Before exploring the relationship between sophomores' plans to take the SAT and their growth in mathematics by the time they graduate from high school, we need to explore who is more likely to have those plans. Sophomores' plans to take the SAT are compared by students' educational aspirations, their parents' education levels, their race or ethnicity, and their mathematics courses and grades. Who plans to take the SAT is an important question, because the answer suggests who would be expected to find the SAT most salient to their future plans, and what obstacles they would have to overcome to perform well on the examination. Since students vary in their expectations about attending college, the set of students planning to take the SAT would be expected to vary similarly. However, this section will show that a substantial percentage of students who might not be expected to attend college still report plans as sophomores to take the SAT.

Figure 6.1 shows that students' plans to take the SAT are related to their own educational expectations, as well as to how far in school their parents went. As might be expected, the percentage of students planning to take the SAT climbs steadily as students expect to go further in school (the white bars in Figure 6.1). About 16% of students who report that they do not plan to continue their education past high school still say they plan to take the SAT. The vast majority (86%) of those sophomores expecting to attend graduate or professional school report planning to take the SAT. However, Figure 6.1 also shows that plans to take the SAT are only partially determined by students' educational aspirations. Some students who plan to attend graduate school do not plan to take the SAT. These may be sophomores who are not aware of the examination or who are planning to attend a school which does not require it. Conversely, many students who do not plan to graduate from college still plan to take the examination.[7] These may be sophomores still hoping to go to college, although they do not expect to do so, or they may be planning to attend a competitive, non-academic, postsecondary school requiring SAT scores. The amount of education students' parents have is also related to students' plans to take the SAT, although not as strongly as the students' own educational aspirations. The black bars in Figure 6.1 show that sophomores whose parents did not continue their education past high school are the least likely to plan to take the SAT, while those whose parents finished graduate school are the most likely to do so. Just under half of the students whose parents only finished high school plan to take the SAT, compared to 85% of those whose parents have graduate degrees. These more educated parents may not only have higher educational expectations for their children, but also may have taken the SAT themselves, both of which may contribute to their children's plans to take the SAT.

Sophomores from different racial and ethnic groups might also be expected to vary in their plans to take college entrance examinations. The top panel of Table 6.2 clearly shows that Asian Americans are the most likely to plan to take the SAT, while Hispanics are the least likely to do so. Over 80% of Asian Americans plan to take the SAT, compared to about 65% of African American and white students, and 58% of Hispanics. The similar percentages of African Americans and whites planning to take the SAT are interesting, given the fact that African Americans are less likely to attend colleges or universities (Hauser 1993). A logistic regression examining the odds that sophomores plan to take the SAT showed that African Americans are 1.6 times more likely to plan to take the examination than white students with similar educational expectations, and social and educational backgrounds. We will return to this puzzle in the discussion section of this chapter.

What mathematics courses students took by their sophomore year and the grades they received are highly related to their plans to take the SAT. The middle panel of Table 6.2 shows that students who have taken at least Algebra II or Geometry by 10th grade are over 30% more likely to plan to take the SAT than sophomores who took neither of those classes. Sophomores who have taken both Algebra II and Geometry (85.9%) are almost twice as likely as students who have taken only Algebra I or General Mathematics courses (45%) to plan to take the SAT. However, nearly half of the sophomores who have not taken the mathematics courses needed to do well on the SAT, and thus, are not positioned in the

TABLE 6.2 Sophomores' Plans to Take the SAT by Their
Race or Ethnicity, and Mathematics Classes and Grades by
Tenth Grade

	Plans to Take the SAT	
	Yes	*No*
Race/Ethnicity		
African American	65.1%	34.9%
Asian American	81.4%	18.6%
Hispanic	58.1%	41.9%
White	65.9%	34.1%
High school mathematics classes by tenth grade		
Algebra I or General Math Only	45.0%	55.0%
Algebra II or Geometry	72.2%	27.8%
Algebra II and Geometry, or Advanced Mathematics	85.9%	14.1%
Mathematics grades in ninth and tenth grades		
Lower than straight Cs	46.3%	53.7%
Some Cs and Bs	63.8%	36.2%
B+ or better	74.4%	25.6%

Source: NELS:88-94 base year and first follow-up.

mathematics sequence to do so before graduating, still plan to take the
examination.

Similarly, sophomores who receive better grades in their mathematics
courses are also more likely to report that they are planning to take the
examination (bottom panel of Table 6.2). Almost three out of every four

sophomores who received grades of B+ or better plan to take the SAT, compared to about 46% of students who received GPAs of C or below. Again, however, almost half of the sophomores who would not be expected to attend college -- in this case, students with low GPAs -- still plan to take the SAT.

These results indicate that a large proportion of American high school sophomores plan to take the SAT. This is true regardless of whether they are planning to or would be expected to attend a four-year college or university. These results suggest that the SAT is salient for many different types of students, and not just for those with the ambition, ability, or resources to attend the most competitive colleges or universities.

Relationships Between College Entrance
Examinations and Mathematics Achievement

If college entrance examinations are an incentive for achievement, differences in mathematics achievement growth should be particularly clear during the last two years of high school. This is the period during which most students take the SAT. If they have not already done so, students need to take the courses and master the curricular material required to do well on the examination. In addition, sophomores with low grades are running out of time to raise their GPAs to the level desired by many postsecondary schools. Doing well on the SAT may help offset some low high school grades in the college admissions process.

Four regression models are used in Table 6.3 to show how sophomores' plans to take the SAT are related to growth in mathematics achievement, controlling on an increasing variety of background and schooling factors. The analyses begin with a base model that includes the sophomore test score and a student's plans to take the SAT. This model sets a baseline difference in academic growth between sophomores who did or did not plan to take the SAT. The next model shows how the effects of test taking plans on mathematics achievement are affected by sophomores' background characteristics. This allows us to determine what portion of the growth in mathematics can be explained by the fact that socially advantaged students are more likely to plan to take the SAT. Model III explores how students' mathematics courses and grades during the first two years of high school also affect the relationship between sophomores' test plans and mathematics achievement. The last model shows how much of the difference between students who do or do not plan to take the SAT is due to differences in their educational expectations.

TABLE 6.3 OLS Regressions of Senior Mathematics Test Scores

Variables	Regression Coefficients			
	Model I	Model II	Model III	Model IV
Sophomore Mathematics Test Scores	1.068***	1.076***	1.067***	1.046***
Mathematics Test Scores Squared	-.001***	-.002***	-.002***	-.002***
Sophomore plans to take SAT	1.337***	1.298***	1.000***	.639***
Background Characteristics				
Male		1.108***	1.212***	1.294***
Parents' Education		.219***	.207***	.166***
Log of Family Income		.074	.086	.046
African American		-.528**	-.679***	-.833***
Asian American		.914**	.760**	.723*
Hispanic		.179	.037	-.076
9th and 10th Mathematics Grades			.425***	.393***
High School Mathematics Courses by Tenth Grade				
Algebra II and Geometry, or Advanced Mathematics			.596***	.565***
Algebra I or General Math Only			-1.339***	-1.174***
Sophomore Educational Expectations				.507***
Constant	3.670	2.190	1.831	1.438
R-Square	.843	.847	.851	.852

*** = p < .001   ** = p < .01   * = p < .05

The first column in Table 6.3 contains the regression equation for Model I, which shows that planning to take the SAT is related to higher mathematics growth. Sophomores who planned to take the SAT gained 1.337 questions more correct by the time they were seniors than students who did not plan to take it. This difference is highly statistically significant and accounts for about 5% of the variation in senior test scores explained by the model (Table 6.A.2 contains the standardized coefficients from the regression equations in Table 6.3).

Is a difference of 1.337 questions substantively or meaningfully significant? One way to answer this question is to compare the difference between students who did or did not plan to take the SAT with differences between types of students (e.g., males and females) that are generally considered to have significant disparities in mathematics achievement. For this purpose, differences between males and females and between racial or ethnic groups were estimated using regression equations (one for gender and another for racial/ethnic groups) in which indicators for each were substituted for "plans to take the SAT." Results show that the difference in mathematics growth between sophomores who planned or did not plan to take the SAT is larger than the differences in growth between males and females (1.05 questions), and between white students and African Americans (.48 questions), and between white students and Asian Americans (1.20 questions). Based on this, we argue that the difference between students who did or did not plan to take the SAT can be considered substantively, in addition to statistically, significant.

Model II shows that the effects of plans to take the SAT are reduced when sophomores' social backgrounds are taken into account. Sophomores who planned to take the SAT gained 1.298 questions more by the time they were seniors than students who did not plan to take the examination. This coefficient is slightly reduced from Model I, yet remains highly significant. SAT plans (Beta = .045) are more influential than any of the background characteristics, even the most influential ones of male (Beta = .040) and parents' education (Beta = .038). The difference between students who plan and do not plan to take the SAT is larger than that between any of the minorities and white students. The difference between African American and white students is just over half a question, compared to a difference of more than a question between students who vary in their plans to take the SAT.

Freshman and sophomore mathematics courses and grades account for about a fifth of the effect of plans to take the SAT on mathematics achievement growth. In Model III, sophomores who planned to take the SAT gained a question more than students who did not plan to take it. While the coefficient is reduced by just under .3 questions between Models

II and III, the effect size is still larger than differences between minorities and whites. Mathematics grades and courses, however, are slightly more influential than students' test plans. Grades account for about 6% of the variation explained by the model, compared to 3% for SAT plans. The difference between sophomores who had taken either Algebra II or Geometry and those who had taken neither of those courses (-1.174) is greater in magnitude than the difference between students who did or did not plan to take the SAT.

Adding sophomores' educational expectations in Model IV sharply reduces the effect of students' plans to take the SAT on mathematics achievement. The coefficient is reduced to just over two-thirds of a question in Model IV from a question in Model III. The coefficient for students' plans is now smaller and less influential than some indicators of students' backgrounds. For example, the difference between African American and white students (.833 of a question) is now larger than that between students who do or do not plan to take the SAT (.639 of a question).[8] However, the effects of plans to take the SAT remain large and highly significant.

The other coefficients in Model IV are consistent with relationships commonly seen in regressions predicting growth between 10th and 12th grades. Parents' education, mathematics grades, educational aspirations, and taking college preparatory mathematics courses are all positively related to mathematics achievement growth. African Americans and students who have taken only basic mathematics courses (Algebra I and General Mathematics) show lower growth rates than other students. It should be noted that factors related to a higher likelihood of planning to take the SAT are also related to higher mathematics achievement growth. Yet, plans to take the SAT remain an important indicator of higher achievement growth. This suggests that there may be an interaction effect between SAT plans and these factors, which will be explored in the next section.

The results in this section indicate that sophomores' plans to take the SAT are significantly related to higher mathematics achievement growth during the last two years of high school. The effects of these plans are attenuated by educational expectations, background characteristics, and how well a student is doing in the subject. Yet, they remain significant and substantial. Thus, an orientation toward taking the SAT seems to be related to higher mathematics growth, independent of students' educational aspirations, social backgrounds, and prior academic preparation and success. This may indicate that the examination is acting as an incentive for higher mathematics achievement. To explore this further, the next section examines whether the effects of plans to take the

SAT differ for groups that may have reasons to feel a greater or lesser incentive to get high scores.

Variations Between Types of Students in the Effects of College Entrance Examinations

The college entrance examinations used to evaluate American high school graduates may not provide the same type or level of incentive for all students. This section explores whether sophomores' plans to take the SAT have varying effects on mathematics growth for different types of students. Five groups of characteristics are examined more closely: students with varying post high school plans; those whose parents have more or less schooling; various racial and ethnic groups; students who have taken different mathematics courses; and those who have received higher or lower mathematics grades.

The tables in this section contain only coefficients for plans to take the SAT from regression equations estimated separately for each group.[9] The coefficients show the difference between sophomores who planned or did not plan to take the SAT for a particular group, taking into account students' social and academic backgrounds along with their educational aspirations. These coefficients can be compared between mutually exclusive groups of students (for example, students who took both Algebra II and Geometry compared to those who took neither of those two courses) to show variations in the effects of planning to take the SAT.

Variations in Effects by Educational Plans for
After High School and Parents' Education

The first of the tables in this section shows how the effect of planning to take the SAT varies among students who differ in their educational aspirations and how far in school their parents went.

The top panel of Table 6.4 shows that plans to take the SAT are most strongly related to growth in mathematics for students who do not plan to graduate from college. In this group, students who plan to take the SAT gain just over a question more than those who did not plan to take it. Students' plans also accounted for about 4% of the variation in senior mathematics test scores explained by the regression model. The coefficients for sophomores' plans to take the SAT are small (close to or less than half a question) and not statistically significant for students planning to graduate from college and those planning to attend graduate school. This indicates that plans to take the SAT are only significantly related to growth in mathematics for students who see graduation from college as questionable.

TABLE 6.4 Differences in the Effects of Sophomores' Plans to Take the SAT on Mathematics Growth by Twelfth Grade by Sophomores' Educational Expectations and Parents' Education

	Regression Coefficients	
	Raw	*Standardized*
Sophomores' Educational Expectations		
Less than graduate from college	1.070***	.043
Graduate from college	.377	.013
Attend graduate or professional school	.538	.015
Parents' Education		
High school or less	.759**	.029
Some postsecondary education	.586**	.021
College graduate	.637*	.021

*** = p < .001   ** = p < .01   * = p < .05

Planning to take the SAT is also related to increased growth in mathematics for students whose parents did not attend college (bottom panel of Table 6.4). In this group, students who plan to take the SAT gain over three-quarters of a question more correct than students who did not plan to take the examination, and this explains about 3% of the variation in senior mathematics test scores accounted for by the regression model. Plans to take the SAT are also significantly related to growth in mathematics for students whose parents attended or graduated from college. However, the difference between students who did or did not plan to take the SAT is much smaller (around .6 questions) for these groups, compared to those whose parents did not attend college.

These results show that sophomores' educational expectations and their parents' education have a similar relationship with the effect of plans to take the SAT on mathematics achievement growth. Plans to take the SAT

TABLE 6.5 Differences in the Effects of Sophomores' Plans to Take the SAT on Mathematics Growth by Twelfth Grade by Students' Race/Ethnicity.

	Regression Coefficients	
Race/Ethnicity	*Raw*	*Standardized*
African American	.154	.006
Asian American	2.100**	.059
Hispanic	.050	.002
White	.751***	.027

are most strongly related to growth in mathematics for students whose educational expectations and parental education would make them seem least likely to take it, that is, those students who do not plan to graduate from college and whose parents did not attend college.

Variations in Effects Between Racial and Ethnic Groups

Although the majority of sophomores from all four racial and ethnic groups plan to take the SAT, it was shown earlier in this chapter that there is substantial variation in the percentages from each group with those plans, with Asians the most likely to plan to take the SAT and Hispanics the least likely. Table 6.5 clearly shows that the effect of plans to take the SAT also varies among ethnic and racial groups.

The most striking results are for Asian American students, for whom sophomore plans to take the SAT are related to gains of just over 2 questions more correct compared to those who did not. For Asian Americans, this growth rate is higher than that associated with any of the other variables, including mathematics course taking and grades. White students also show a significant effect for plans to take the SAT, but the difference between whites who do and do not plan to take the SAT is less than half that for Asian American students with or without those plans. White sophomores who planned to take the SAT gained about .75 questions more correct than those who did not. The results for Hispanic and African American students show that plans to take the SAT are not related to increased growth in mathematics for these groups.[10] The coefficients are very small, not statistically significant, and account for virtually none of the variation in senior mathematics test scores accounted for by the model.

This pattern presents somewhat of a puzzle compared to the other student background characteristics, since it is not those who are least likely to attend college who show the most growth when they plan to take the SAT. This may partly be due to differences in the way Hispanic and African American students are advised about college attendance. As noted earlier, African American sophomores are almost twice as likely to plan to take the SAT than whites with similar social and academic backgrounds. This may account for the lower correlation between sophomore mathematics test scores and plans to take the SAT for African Americans ($r = .28$), compared to whites ($r = .36$). The pattern gets even more complex after comparing African American and white students who *took* the SAT in contrast to those *planning* to do so.[11] African Americans who planned to take the SAT but did not follow through on it had lower mathematics growth rates compared to whites who similarly changed their minds. Possibly more telling, African Americans who planned to take the SAT and followed through on those plans had higher growth rates compared to whites, regardless of their plans and whether they took the examination. One possible explanation is that high school counselors may "cool out" African American students' educational aspirations later than they do so for white students. Thus, may encourage academically weak African American sophomores to consider attending college, but later advise them to adjust those plans if their achievement does not improve during the last two years of high school.

Variations in Effects by Mathematics Courses and Grades

The effect of plans to take the SAT on mathematics achievement also varies by the types of mathematics courses students took as freshmen and sophomores, and the grades they received in those classes.

The top panel of Table 6.6 shows that sophomores who planned to take the SAT had the greatest relative growth if they had taken neither Algebra II nor Geometry, which are two classes they need to do well on the SAT. For this group, students who plan to take the SAT gain over a question more correct than those who do not have those plans. This difference accounts for about 5% of the variation in senior test scores explained by the regression model. Plans to take the SAT do not significantly affect mathematics growth for students who had taken either Algebra II or Geometry, or both classes.

The bottom panel of Table 6.6 shows that plans to take the SAT are most highly related to growth in mathematics for students whose grades are borderline for getting into college (the middle category). Those students

TABLE 6.6 Differences in the Effects of Sophomores' Plans to Take the SAT on Mathematics Growth by Twelfth Grade by Mathematics Classes and Grades by Tenth Grade

	Regression Coefficients	
	Raw	Standardized
High School Mathematics Classes by Tenth Grade		
Algebra I or General Math Only	1.012***	.046
Algebra II or Geometry	.366	.016
Algebra II and Geometry, or Advanced Mathematics	.460	.014
Mathematics Grades in Ninth and Tenth Grades		
Lower than Straight Cs	.556	.024
Some Cs and Bs	.898***	.035
B+ or better	.286	.010

*** = p < .001   ** = p < .01   * = p < .05

whose freshman and sophomore mathematics grades are a mixture of Bs and Cs gain .898 questions more correct if they plan to take the SAT than if they do not. This accounts for about 3% of the explained variance in the model. Plans to take the SAT are not related to differences in mathematics growth for students whose average mathematics grades are lower than straight Cs, and whose grades are B+ or better. For the latter, their grades should be high enough to provide fairly easy admission to all but very competitive schools. For the former, their grades are so low that it would be difficult to raise them high enough for entrance to any school, except one with open admissions. Even high SAT scores would be unlikely to help these students' chances of admission to more competitive schools.

As before, the results from Table 6.6 indicate that students who might not be expected to attend college seem to show higher growth if they planned as sophomores to take the SAT. Students who have not taken college preparatory mathematics courses or whose grades are borderline for getting into college seem to gain more in mathematics if they plan to take the SAT, compared to similar students who do not plan to take the examination.

Conclusions: Implications for Incentive Systems

In summary, this chapter started by showing that plans to take the SAT are very common among American high school sophomores. Even some students who do not think they will attend college report planning to take this examination. This is also true for students who might be expected for various reasons not to attend college, such as students who have not taken college preparatory mathematics courses by the end of 10th grade, those who have not received high grades in mathematics during the first two years of high school, those whose parents did not finish college, and racial or ethnic minorities. Even among these students for whom college attendance is questionable, half to two-thirds of them still plan to take the SAT.

The analyses show that sophomores' plans to take the SAT have implications for their academic achievement. Students who plan to take the SAT have significantly higher growth in mathematics achievement by their senior year than their classmates who did not plan to take the examination. This is true when controlling on their prior achievement, social background, and educational expectations, along with mathematics courses taken and grades received during the first two years of high school. The results also show that plans t take the SAT have their greatest effect on students who may be considered educationally disadvantaged, such as those whose parents did not have any postsecondary education, those who had taken neither Algebra II nor Geometry by 10th grade, and those whose grades were borderline for college entrance. Exceptions to this trend are the lack of an effect of plans to take the SAT on achievement for African American and Hispanic students, and large effects for Asian Americans. Thus, planning to take the SAT may have clear consequences for students, although how strongly those consequences are felt, seems to vary for different types of students.

We argue that these results suggest that the SAT may provide some students with an incentive to increase their mathematics achievement. Drawing on these results, we suggest that four factors need to be considered when designing incentive systems based on external examinations. For the purposes of this discussion, we call these factors "information, salience, legitimacy, and effort." We argue that all four of these factors must be taken into account when designing effective incentive systems.

Information: Effects of Knowledge of an Incentive System

On a very basic level, if a student is not aware of an evaluation, then there is no way it can affect his or her actions.   The importance of information, however, is more complex, since access to information may be more important for some students than for others.   The results in this chapter concerning the interaction between parents' education and sophomores' plans to take the SAT illustrate this issue. For students whose parents did not attend college, those with plans to take the SAT may have a greater awareness of what it takes to get into college than do students with similar backgrounds who do not plan to take the examination. One advantage students have, whose parents who went to college, is that they are likely to pass on to them knowledge of how non-academic factors, such as participation in extracurricular activities, may influence college admissions decisions. Thus, for an incentive to be effective, those whom it is designed to motivate must be aware of it. This awareness may be more crucial for students who lack other incentives or environmental support for high academic achievement.

Salience: Effects of the Importance of Success

Even if students know about an examination, it may fail to motivate them to work harder if they do not view their performance as important for their future. This salience may come from students' desires to estimate their likelihood of success in college, or a need to demonstrate to others that they are capable of that success. The first may explain the variations in the effects of plans to take the SAT by students' educational expectations. For those students who have doubts about whether they will graduate from college, doing well on the SAT may be crucial. These students may use success on this examination as a gauge for whether or not they should attend college (Jencks and Crouse 1982; Slack and Porter 1980). This is one of the Educational Testing Service's stated purposes of the SAT (Crouse and Trusheim 1988). Thus, students who lacked confidence that they would graduate from college may find encouragement to pursue higher education if they perform well on the SAT.

The second aspect of salience may explain the curve linear relationship between the effect of plans to take the SAT and students' mathematics grades. Those students with borderline grades show the greatest response to the prospect of taking the SAT, compared to those with very low or high grades. These students may have greater incentives to perform on the SAT as a means of offsetting or augmenting their borderline grades in the eyes of admission personnel. Students whose grades are higher do not need added evidence from test scores to obtain admission to the school of their choice, while those whose grades are lower than Cs are unlikely to be admitted to selective schools even if they had high test scores.

In other countries with strong external examination systems, grades and test scores take on different meanings then in the U.S. As noted earlier, many American students depend on their high school grades rather than their SAT scores to get them admitted to the college of their choice. This is in stark contrast to the Japanese and German systems, where how well students perform on college entrance examinations determines which school, if any, they will attend (Eckstein and Noah 1993). In these countries, grades are not used externally to evaluate students. Instead, they provide students with indicators of how well they can expect to do on the examinations (Kariya and Rosenbaum 1987). Grades work to reinforce the salience of these college entrance examinations, rather than acting as a separate indicator of a student's achievement.

Legitimacy: Effects of Believing the Evaluation Is Fair

Students may know about an examination and understand its importance, but still decide against making an effort to perform well if they think the examination does not provide them with a fair opportunity for success. The variations in effects of plans to take the SAT between ethnic and racial groups may reflect differences in how the examinations are viewed. Asian Americans, among whom the greatest effect of plans to take the SAT is found, may be influenced by the experiences of parents or other family members in a school system, such as those in Japan and China, where test scores are the sole determinant of attendance in higher education (Stevenson and Baker 1992). The lack of an effect of plans to take the SAT among African American students may reflect a different view of standardized tests, namely that they are a mechanism of institutional discrimination. African Americans have historically not performed as well on standardized tests, especially the SAT, as white students. Only a small number of African Americans would attend college if their admission was based solely on SAT scores (Crouse and Trusheim 1988).[12] African American students may be well aware of charges that these examinations discriminate against them (Jencks and Crouse 1982), and thus, may not view them as a legitimate means of evaluation. These differences in the effects of plans to take the SAT among racial and ethnic groups suggest that for an external evaluation system to provide incentives, it must be viewed as legitimate and fair.

Effort: Effects of Needing to Struggle for Success

Knowledge of an evaluation and its importance for students' futures may fail to act as an incentive for some students if performing well on the examination does not require much effort on their part. This is clearly shown by variations in the effects of plans to take the SAT by the mathematics courses students took as freshmen and sophomores. Plans to take the SAT seem to provide a greater incentive for students who are less prepared for the examination. Those who have had neither Algebra II nor Geometry by 10th grade have much curricular material to cover in order to do well on the examination. For sophomores who have already had both these subjects, the SAT does not present as much of an incentive to study mathematics. Thus, for an incentive to be effective, it must require effort from those hoping to reach the desired goal.

In summary, this chapter suggests that for an incentive system to be effective, individuals must be aware of the examination, see doing well on it as a goal to strive toward, and feel attainment of that goal is important. Also, these factors are necessary, but not sufficient, to motivate action, if the evaluation system is not viewed as legitimate or fair. This means that the SAT may provide incentives for higher academic achievement for some students, but not for others. Examples of the first are those students for whom college attendance may be problematic due to a lack of resources or mediocre academic records. Examples of the second are those students with very strong or very weak academic records, and those whose parents attended college themselves. This suggests that when designing an incentive system, the social situations and characteristics of the individuals the system is designed to motivate must be carefully considered. Particularly important is having externally established evaluations and standards that are tied to clear consequences. It is not the advantaged students, either socially or academically, who benefit most from such an incentive system. Instead, the system seems to assist most those who lack other incentives or encouragements for high performance.

Notes

1. The analyses are weighted to be representative of the 1988 eighth grade cohort. The weights provided in F2PNLWT are standardized as directed in NCES (1994).

2. The questionnaire also asked about the other major college entrance examination used in the U.S., the American College Test (ACT). Preliminary analyses included indicators for plans to take the ACT, but they were dropped from the models for two reasons. First, only 5% of all students planned to take *only* the ACT. Second, effects for plans to take only the ACT were small and not significantly different from planning to take neither of the examinations. These results did not change even after controlling on the region of the country.

3. Similar analyses were performed with the other subject tests in NELS:88-94 (English, History/Social Studies, and Science) and the results were substantively the same.

4. The senior mathematics test score, rather than the difference between the sophomore and senior test scores, is used as the dependent variable because they are easier to interpret. The coefficient for the sophomore mathematics test score reflects the difference, or growth, between sophomore and senior test scores. The coefficients for the other variables measure additional changes in senior test scores, after taking into account changes due to level of performance on the sophomore tests.

5. American Indians were not included in these analyses because the number in the sample is very small, making group estimates questionable.

6. Close to 30% of students change their educational expectations across the four years of high school. Also, those students who did not plan to graduate from college are the most likely to change their expectations, usually toward higher expectations.

7. It is not the case that students with lower educational expectations plan to take the ACT instead of the SAT. The percentage of students planning to take only the ACT remains fairly constant across all levels of educational aspirations.

8. One interesting pattern in Table 6.3 shows that as courses, grades, and aspirations are added to the models, the effect of African American gets larger, growing from -.528 to -.833. This may suggest that their grades, course placements, and educational expectations are not related to their mathematics achievement in ways that these factors are for other types of students.

9. Control variables used for Model IV in Table 6.3 are included in these models where appropriate. The regression models for mutually exclusive groups (e.g., mathematics courses categories of Algebra I or General Mathematics, Algebra II or Geometry, and Algebra II and Geometry) are mathematically equivalent models run for the entire sample with interaction terms between group indicators and all the other variables in the equation. The complete regression equations for Tables 6.4 to 6.6 are shown in Appendix Tables 6.A.3a to 6.A.5b.

10. Regressions were run including school-level measures of the percentage of African Americans and the percentage of graduates who go on to four-year colleges, but the effects for plans to take the SAT were unchanged.

11. The change in average mathematics test scores between 10th and 12th grades for the four groups discussed in this paragraph are: (1) whites who planned and took the SAT = 5.0; (2) whites who planned to take the SAT but did not = 4.3; (3) African Americans who planned and took the SAT = 3.6; and (4) African Americans who planned to but did not take the SAT = 5.2.

12. Crouse and Trusheim (1991) note that many universities and colleges, even selective ones, do not require SAT scores from African American applicants. If they do, many postsecondary schools give the scores a different weight than for white students. This suggests that a lack of salience may also contribute to the lack of an effect for plans to take the SAT among African Americans and Hispanics. The large effect of Asian Americans and differences between African Americans who do or do not take the examination, however, support the contention that the perceived legitimacy of the examination may affect how hard students work in school in order to do well on the examination.

7

Prognosis for Reform: Lessons from an Output-Driven Educational System

Barbara Schneider

A series of principles derived from the output-driven system model have been discussed that when employed can create a force for energizing and focusing student and teacher actions. The principles are based on an understanding of schools as social systems requiring strong norms of academic achievement if productivity is to increase. Such norms can be strengthened by establishing standards that reinforce high achievement and incentives that reward student performance. While our empirical work cannot directly test whether such a system would dramatically change the productivity of American schools, we have shown that there are conditions that appear quite promising for raising academic performance.

An output-driven system depends on several requisite conditions. First, the public school system needs to be reorganized in substantial ways-- schools need to be smaller, and parents should be encouraged to select their children's school. Second, standards and incentive systems that reward high academic performance and are external to individual schools and districts must be put in place. Third, the professional role of the teacher needs to be redefined from evaluator to coach with teachers no longer grading students but rather assisting students in mastering the knowledge and skills defined by external standards.

Positive Effects of Output-Driven Principles

Our empirical results indicate that student performance is likely to increase when academic values and incentives are central to a school's organizational culture. When schools direct their activities toward the pursuit of academic excellence, students have higher levels of performance than students in schools that do not. This achievement effect is especially strong in schools where the majority of students are from poor families or have parents with low levels of education. Additionally, in schools where poverty is accompanied by absent or weak norms that stress academic press, a strong sense of community is associated with lower levels of academic achievement.

One could envision a school that would establish practices designed to increase the opportunity of all students to become academically engaged. One such practice would be to require all students to take mainstream academic subjects. In mathematics, for example, instead of shuttling less able students into remedial courses, the output-driven school would demand that they learn algebra. Similar arrangements could be made for other subject areas. All students, for instance, might be expected to learn at least the basics of a foreign language with the option to go even further. Although some students might need two years to learn what other students could learn in one semester, all students would travel the same learning path.

This type of common academic agenda would not only promote more equal educational opportunity, but would also signify a belief that higher-order knowledge is appropriate for all students. Cohesive social relations would serve to reinforce these values as students work together to overcome obstacles and meet common goals. A common academic agenda runs counter to arguments that curriculum and instruction should be tailored to the diverse needs and interests of individuals, and that students should have a major say in determining what they will learn and how they will learn it. Yet, it is an idea quite consistent with an understanding of the school as a shaping institution that directs its resources to helping students acquire specific knowledge and skills. In a real sense, the output-driven school sends a message to its potential members: "This is what we are about, and we invite you to join our learning community."

Norms that stress academic achievement can be a social resource for schools, families, and students, upon which the foundation for a meaningful school community can be built. We maintain that an authentic sense of community develops as individuals work toward removing hurdles that interfere with common goals. When these work activities center around academic effort and learning, schools can become viable communities. When they do not, people may justly begin to question what compelling or enduring purpose is served through the creation of schools, let alone through the creation of school communities.

Our argument is not intended to detract from the importance of communality, but, rather to clarify its basis and development. There are two troubling misconceptions which often characterize much of the schools as communities literature. The first of these is that developing a school's sense of community is mainly a matter of adopting communal characteristics and behaviors (Lightfoot 1983; Power, Higgens and Kohlberg 1989). The second is that developing a community constitutes a key purpose, rather than a key process of schooling (Powell, Farrar and Cohen 1985; Sergiovanni 1994). Neither of these views of schools as communities adequately stress that a community with strong norms for academic achievement develops from members working toward the collective goals of academic excellence and learning.

Some supporters of communality assert that each school community should develop its own set of performance goals, that schools must be more responsive to local needs, and that shared decisionmaking about curricular activities allows teachers more responsibility in school operations and parents more direct involvement with significant school matters (Bryk and Rollow 1992; Cors 1991; Darling-Hammond 1995; NASSP 1992; Whelage, Rutter, Smith, Lesko and Fernandez 1989). However, our results strongly indicate that limiting the control teachers have over curricular content while granting teachers a high level of autonomy in determining teaching techniques is more beneficial for raising student achievement. Placing control of curricular content outside of an individual teacher's discretion lessens the chance that major curricular topics will not be covered and enhances the probability that topics will be taught sequentially from year to year. Externally derived curricular decisions allow teachers more time and opportunities to fine-tune their instruction and structure their classroom environments to suit the academic needs of their students. This type of pedagogical freedom facilitates teachers' efforts to motivate students to behave well and work hard which results in high achievement.

The academically oriented output-driven school represents far more than a "return to the basics." With teams of teachers working in a collegial fashion, sharing responsibilities for instructional design, students are likely to be exposed to a wide variety of classroom experiences. Learning would thus occur through a blend of tradition and innovation; through lecture, discussion, and recitation, as well as through cooperative activities and hands-on projects. Faced with incentives to teach students, rather than to explain why certain students could not be taught, teachers would design ways to "loop" or "spiral" students through previously unlearned material.[1]

In these types of learning situations where the teachers take on the role of academic coach, the teachers could more easily emphasize and establish a spirit of teamwork and healthy competitiveness. If teachers are not giving grades, students will be less likely to spend energy attempting to bargain or to ingratiate themselves with their teachers in order to get higher grades. Instead of close contact between teacher and student being seen merely as a route to getting higher grades, such contact is desired because it increases the chances of learning the material. It is not out of bounds or "uncool" to ask and expect that the teacher will help one learn complicated material.

Finally we wanted to look at the impact external standards might have on student performance. Unfortunately with our data sets, we were unable to determine which of the schools were located in states with external standards. Consequently, we used the Scholastic Aptitude Test (SAT) as a proxy for an externally controlled exam with high stakes results. The SAT is being increasingly relied upon for college admissions because college admission officers have less confidence in their own abilities to evaluate high school transcripts or grade point averages (Worthington 1996). Specifically, we examined what effect taking the SAT had on student achievement growth in mathematics.

Our analyses clearly demonstrate that among high school seniors who reported planning to take the SAT as sophomores, their mathematics test scores were nearly an average ten percent higher than seniors who did not have such plans as sophomores. The effect of planning to take the SAT remains robust even when taking into account students' social backgrounds, success in school, and educational expectations. The increases in mathematics achievement were generally highest among those students for whom college attendance may be difficult, such as those whose grades are borderline "passing" or who have not taken college preparatory mathematics courses.

These results indicate that when designing a performance assessment system based on external examinations, the results of the exams must have real consequences for the students' future life opportunities. Although such high stakes external examination models have been criticized for being inequitable and unnecessarily stressful (Crouse and Trusheim 1991), we would argue that if the scores have limited consequences for the students, then the students are much less likely to take them seriously. An example of what happens when students see such external testing as inconsequential was recently reported in city-wide testing in Chicago (Brodt 1996). Another example is in Kentucky, where the state had to change its accountability testing from 12th to 11th grade because many 12th grade students were not taking or finishing the tests because the results were returned too late to influence graduation or college admission decisions.

If school systems move toward requiring high stakes external examinations, we would strongly recommend that all students receive equal opportunities to learn the content and consequences of the exams and that major resources be devoted to assist students to adequately prepare for such examinations. Presently, as our results indicate, students with considerable family and school resources are the most informed, and activities by the school do not affect their performance. This is not the case for students with limited family and school resources. For such students, information and preparation are necessities.

Examples of Output-Driven Principles in Practice

We argue that our empirical findings are supported by more than large-scale data analyses. Several of the current educational reforms in the U.S. exemplify various components of output-driven principles. Many of these efforts are small localized school initiatives, while others have been adopted at a state level. Preliminary results from some of these efforts complement our empirical findings. We review several of these programs which suggest how output-driven principles can be used to promote organizational change with surprisingly positive outcomes.

Central Park East
Perhaps one of the best examples of how output-driven principles can be used at the school level is Central Park East in New York's East Harlem, which was founded by Deborah Meier (1995)[2]. Comprised of four public schools of choice working in close collaboration with each other, the educational programs and outcomes in this group of schools stand in sharp contrast to those commonly associated with inner city public schools. With a predominately low-income minority population of African American and Latino students, this group of schools keeps nearly all of its student body in school and in 1994 graduated a high school class from which over 90 percent entered postsecondary schools.

From its very beginning in 1974, the philosophy of Central Park East reflected the normative concept of Coleman's output-driven system. Meier envisioned a school in which people found voice in their own work and the work of others. There would be no "us" versus "them," but rather a unified working collaborative where the overriding ideology was that urban children could learn and that low and trivial expectations for them were unacceptable. These expectations were not global platitudes but real guides for action that required the commitment of all school personnel, parents, and students.

Through the years, a value system has developed where teachers and students are committed to treating their work as serious and consequential. Mutual respect among the teachers, families, and students is central, and a climate of diversity is encouraged. Students are expected to take responsibility for who they are and what they can accomplish.

Recognizing that the school and families will be very supportive of students' efforts, the school takes the position that the students must be primarily responsible for their own performance.

Such an environment is sustainable in large part because of the organizational structure of the schools. Choice for public school parents is a major strength. According to Meier, a crucial factor in the school's success is that families are electing to place their children in an environment where they think the children would succeed. The teachers, parents, and students see the school as theirs. Ownership is a key element of the model which reinforces a sense of membership in a community, a quality that many families living in high poverty areas are missing in their lives.

School size is another key organizational factor for enhancing student productivity. The total Central Park East enrollment consists of approximately 250 students in each of the three elementary schools and 450 students in grades seven through twelve, numbers which would be considered small by nearly all standards. Schools of this size can more easily facilitate the establishment of relationships among school staff, students and families, than schools where enrollments run over 1,000 students. Small schools tend to allow more opportunities for frequent communication and the building of shared beliefs of what constitutes a high quality educational program (Lee and Smith 1995).

Creating smaller and more focused educational communities can enhance the ties among families, teachers, and students that lead to greater trust (Bryk, Lee and Holland 1993). In Central Park East, relationships are further strengthened because the teachers keep their students for two years[3]. Having the same students for more than one year provides the teachers with the opportunity to really know what their students are capable of doing and how to help them. Small schools can also help with teacher accountability. In a small school, everyone knows who is late, who is unprepared, and who is doing a good job. Faculty are held responsible for their work and that of their colleagues.

The assessment of students at Central Park East High School is performed by an external review team of college faculty, teachers from other schools, and in some instances students. Non-traditional measures of evaluation are used, such as portfolios, which students present to the Graduation Committee for questioning and defense. Tapes of these sessions are shared with the school staff who also rate the students. Both external raters and staff come together and review their rationale and ratings of the student's work. Meier suggests that this process is a form of publicness where everything is brought before the whole community.

Central Park East exists in a policy environment where its efforts are tolerated but not necessarily supported. State and local systems have permitted Central Park East the opportunity to survive but offer little additional fiscal or human resources that can be used to help the school reach its goals. Because of these circumstances, Central Park East has been forced to take on a wide range of responsibilities some of them extremely burdensome especially with respect to a primary resource, staff time.

To replicate the success of Central Park East among America's 20,000 high schools will require policies that are supportive and that relieve the school of two burdensome tasks; determining what is going to be taught, and an external assessment process. If the overall system were in fact supportive, we would argue that definitions of curriculum content and external assessment could be moved to external agents, and teachers would be free to work more intensively on instruction. Such policies would also help to ensure that when students move from grade to grade, or from school to school, the teacher could have realistic expectations about what the students have been taught.

Charter Schools

Another new form of school organization that exemplifies several principles of an output-driven system is the charter school.[4] Relatively new and growing at an astonishing rate, charter schools are designed to expand educational choice by offering alternatives to standard public school programs. Currently, 25 states have approved charter school legislation. A charter school is an autonomous public school created and operated under a contract between teachers, parents, or others from the public sector with a local school board, state board, or some other public authority. The contract or charter "defines" a charter school, specifying its educational plan, expected outcomes, assessment procedures, management, and compliance with other requirements (Bierlein and Mulholland 1995).

Charter schools vary in their organizational structure, curricular programs, target student populations and school funding. The most defining characteristic of charter schools is that they provide teachers, parents, the community, and administrators the opportunity and flexibility to design their own school structure; for example, graded versus nongraded, selective versus more open admission policies, and curricular focus. The potential difficulty with charter schools is that they are so autonomous that they may educate in ways that do not reflect more broadly based standards.

Charter schools are expected to develop their own standards and are held accountable for student performance. However, as in the instance of Central Park East, these are internally derived standards. If states were to set external standards, charter schools would also be held accountable to the state standards. It seems that the benefit of charter schools from an output-driven perspective is that they allow for choice, direct involvement, and the opportunity to create a normative environment that extols achievement. The only drawback is that without some external standard to hold them to particular performance levels, charter schools may have unknown and highly variable rates of student productivity. We would argue that it is not just flexibility that is lacking in schools but a means to keep them accountable to some standard.

Importance of External Standards

Discussions about the formation of standards are highly contentious (Cohen 1995; Ravitch 1993). The recent passage of Goals 2000: Educate America Act (1994) called for the formation of voluntary state standards, although some policy makers and educators have advocated national standards and national assessments. While moving standards to a national or state level increases the risk of having them become watered-down, it does reduce the risk of schools adopting even lower standards or failing to cover essential material entirely. Critics of national standards suggest that "standard" discussions need to take place at the state or local level and without such dialogue there will be little opportunity for consensus building (Darling-Hammond 1994). Others suggest that Goals 2000 represents the first real bipartisan consensus building around issues of standards and assessment (Stevenson 1995).

At a more generic level, critics of using standards and assessments as mechanisms for school improvement assert that the major problems in schools today are not low expectations and minimal effort by teachers and students. Rather, they contend, the major problems in schools are inadequate resources, poorly prepared teachers, and ineffective classroom practices (Darling-Hammond 1994). But policy decisions need not choose between either the implementation of high stakes assessment or the redistribution of resources. Policy reforms can target both areas simultaneously. The output-driven model urges the implementation of incentive programs that encourage teams of teachers to seek new and more effective classroom practices. The present organization of schools, which offers few rewards for high achievement, inhibits the search for better practices and the desire to achieve academically. There is no simple path from high and external standards to high levels of effort and achievement (Linn 1993). Rather, one important intermediate step is the creation of external standards, in conjunction with other organizational changes, such as providing opportunities for enhancing the professionalism of teaching through more rigorous certification requirements, and incentives for encouraging effective practices.

Giving teachers the primary responsibility for determining what the curriculum should be, rather than an external agent, is problematic for several reasons. First, what is taught in one school may be different than what is taught in another school within the same city. There is little agreement regarding what children should learn, and consequently each part of the education system--be it individual schools, districts, or state systems-may pursue different and sometimes contradictory goals (Ravitch 1993). This makes the sequencing of material in subjects other than mathematics, which has a national hierarchical structure, difficult and for some subjects nearly impossible (Stevenson, Schiller and Schneider 1994). Sequencing issues are especially important given that so many urban school students move and transfer from one school to another, especially today with the increasing possibilities for public school choice (Swanson and Schneider 1996).

Second, external standards and definitions of what should be taught help to build teacher professional normative standards of what constitutes a sound curriculum. Professional norms around standards can help to create a language and set of expectations about what is good practice that can be transferred from one school to the next. What seems vitally important for teachers is that a common vocabulary and understanding of what constitutes good teaching is shared beyond the walls of single schools or teacher networks such as subject matter departments.

Such a general framework for the teaching profession is easier to construct from a curricular-based model. The National Council for the Teachers of Mathematics (NCTM), has in fact begun such a process with the establishment of the mathematics standards curriculum. The mathematics standards provide guides for improving mathematics teaching practices, such as emphasizing the importance of problem-solving rather than rote memorization of all mathematical applications.

New Roles for Teachers

Certainly we need schools where teachers have considerable control over decision making, have frequent opportunities to interact with one another, and are familiar with each other's work. But the amount of discretion teachers currently have over what is taught seems somehow misdirected. It has been argued that determining curricular content is at best tangential to the "particular and characteristic productive agenda" of teaching (Barr and Dreeben 1983). Spending large blocks of time deliberating over what kinds of courses to teach makes it less likely that sufficient time will be devoted to the highly complex task of determining the best ways of instructing students. Thus the most pressing issue, it appears to us, is how to organize and present the content so that students learn in a systematic way.

Several efforts are currently underway to change the role of the teacher. There is growing evidence that teachers have not been adequately prepared to create and conduct valid assessments (Taylor and Nolan 1996). Some of the national professional associations such as NCTM, are developing materials to assist teachers to use more appropriate assessments into their teaching practices (NCTM 1991 and NCTM 1995). Even an output-driven model would suggest that teachers need to engage in continuous diagnostic procedures to ensure that students are learning the specified content. However, from an output-driven perspective these forms of internal classroom assessments should not be tied to grades or other measures of student productivity but instead to indicators of where students are succeeding or having difficulty. The teacher's role should be entirely focused on helping the student grasp the material, not to evaluate his or her performance using some external measure such as letter grades.

The Talent Development Model, a major high school reform initiative is being undertaken by Johns Hopkins University and Howard University that has as one of its objectives to change the role of teacher from evaluator to coach. This effort to redefine the role of teaching is part of a larger project designed to change the high school organization, curriculum, and instruction based upon research on student motivation and teacher commitment. The Talent Development Model emphasizes a college preparatory core curriculum based on high standards and a learning environment that incorporates four sources of student motivation: relevance of schoolwork, a caring and supportive human environment, opportunities for academic success, and help with personal problems (LaPoint, Jordan, McPartland and Towns 1996). Like Central Park East, the Talent model has fostered a small high school environment, in this case by creating schools-within-a school.

From an output-driven perspective, the most interesting aspect of the Talent model is the modification that has been made in teachers' roles and responsibilities. Teachers in the Talent model are expected to coach their students. External departmental exams rather than tests constructed by individual teachers, are used as a major criteria for student grades in each course. Teachers and students know the content of these exams, and know that it is not open to debate or modification. Students pressuring teachers to lower standards shifts to students asking teachers for help in exam preparation. Since the teachers are also being judged by the performance of their students, they have an incentive to place extra effort in helping the students achieve. Thus the focus of the program is having the teacher move from an objective evaluator to a facilitator of student learning.

In many ways, the concept of changing the role of teacher fits well with new theoretical visions of how teachers should teach (Cohen, McLaughlin and Talbert 1993). These new visions of teachers depart from traditional models where teachers transmit knowledge and students repeat it back, and instead describe a dynamic process where, "...teachers function as guides, coaches, and facilitator of students' learning through posing questions, challenging students' thinking and leading them in examining ideas and relationships" (Cohen, McLaughlin and Talbert 1993 p.1). The model is based on the assumption that what students learn has to do fundamentally with how they learn it. Students are not only expected to learn facts but to explore, imagine, reason, formulate and solve problems.

Knowing how to teach in a subject area and within a particular topic area is regarded as an essential element of teaching for understanding. The "teach for understanding" model is especially relevant to the output-driven model, in that the role of the teacher is centered on how to teach, and that teachers and students will work in a close interactive relationship. The model also calls for new strategies of assessment and valuing students' work and progress. Replacing teach and test, the teach for understanding model moves ongoing evaluation of classroom life and student thinking processes as central to teacher practices.

Cohen, Mclaughlin and Talbert (1993) recognize that the expectations and norms of typical American public schools lessen the possibilities for teaching for understanding in many ways. Lack of support from colleagues or from administrators can dampen spirit and initiative. Teachers in such a model have to recognize their own deficiencies, something that even the most self-confident professional is uncomfortable with. Parents, community members, and district personnel may question the value of a curriculum focused on understanding as opposed to more conventional curricular guides.

Despite the conflict that may arise from internal or external forces, the model presents a more learner-centered model which we believe lies at the base of the output-driven model. Teach for understanding is not incompatible with an academic achievement model. We want students to learn, and how they learn should be the most important and basic role of the teacher. One aspect of the teach for understanding model that needs further amplification is the building of norms that bridge parent and teacher interests in achievement with more effective methods for how to accomplish them. A major theme in this chapter has been that transforming the role of the teacher is unlikely to occur without some fundamental change in the incentive structure under which schools and teachers operate. The present typical incentive structures which reward teachers for each additional year of teaching experience and supplemental education credits are basically inconsistent with a system that values growth in student achievement. Research suggests that traditional methods for altering how much we pay teachers will have minimal effects on practice (Lortie 1975; Johnson 1990). The movement is to make teacher salary more aligned with student outcomes, although an integral part of the standards dialogue, teacher compensation has yet to be adopted by states or become part of any major reform effort (Firestone 1994).

Incentives and Rewards

Teachers who are able to do an exceptional job with their students deserve some special kind of recognition in the process. Presently, there are two different types of teacher incentive models that are based on an outcome model. Firestone, (1994) refers to these as individual and collective models. Collective incentive programs tend to reward schools for raising the mean level of the students on standardized achievement tests. South Carolina has developed a plan where student achievement gains in reading and mathematics are the primary criteria, with student attendance and teacher attendance improvements serving as additional criteria for additional awards once achievement gains are realized. Schools are grouped according to student socioeconomic status to make the results more comparable. Awards are distributed to the top 25% of schools in each group and cannot be used as salary but must be put toward instructional materials and equipment. Kentucky and a number of other states are in the process of implementing or experimenting with similar collective incentive programs.

Individual models, that reward individual teachers for raising the performance of their students have received less recognition. An incentive model that rewards teachers on the basis of a value-added model is practically non-existent. Unfortunately, we do not have evaluation data on effects of collective or individual incentive programs for raising student productivity.

The certificates of the National Board for Professional Teaching Standards, can help to provide incentives for some teachers. This new voluntary board awards certificates to teachers who can pass exams that are similar in the extent of specific technical knowledge as those used in the legal or medical profession. The rationale behind a rigorous certification process is that teachers who pass such high-powered tests are "master teachers" and more likely to provide better classroom instruction. While this may be very helpful in distinguishing excellent teachers, we question its applicability for an incentive for improving practice beyond small numbers of professionals. The problem with relying on state programs or national certification to change the system is that these efforts are piecemeal rather than systemic in their approach. Teachers work in school settings where the definition of what constitutes good teaching is often school based. Until there is a normative base which changes how people think about education or its value in American society, we will have a difficult time changing behaviors.

One of the problems with such an output-driven system is that there will be students who will not meet standards, teachers who will be unsuccessful in their efforts to help students learn, and schools that will stay entrenched in poor achievement. A system that demands standards and external measures of assessment nearly ensures that there will be some who will not be able to make the grade. But we must recognize the extent of failure we are willing to tolerate in any educational system. What we currently tolerate may be too great for our system to improve. We need to organize our educational system so that the incentive structure offers positive life chances, for as many students as possible.

Policy makers and scholars continue to believe that the public education system can be changed in meaningful ways that will ultimately make America's schools more productive. Clearly the principles of an output-driven system are worthy of being addressed in the context of school reform initiatives. Practitioners engaging in reform need mechanisms, such as instructional methods, to help ensure higher levels of performance. However, they also need a set of shared understandings about what students should be able to do in school and what role they need to play in helping students achieve those goals. Having clear and shared norms that are widely upheld and reinforced in classroom practices can help to reduce teacher uncertainty of their professional role and instill a stronger sense of institutional purpose among students, parents, and staff. Without such performance norms for students and teachers, it is unlikely that reform practices will be to able accomplish major changes that can be sustained over time.

In this work, we attempted to test various aspects of the output-driven model and relate them to current innovative practices in schools. Continued empirical study that focuses on the underlying aspects of the system that impede academic productivity is needed. One area we need to keep our attention on is the connection between the organization of the schooling system and the organizational norms that promote or constrain its effectiveness. Studying the system holistically allows us to think about how norms between teachers and students are formed. It is the formation of these norms that occur through teacher student interaction that drives the productivity of the educational system.

Notes

1. Looping or spiraling refers to an instrumental process in which knowledge, concepts, and problems presented earlier in a course are continually re-integrated into subsequent lessons so as to offer students numerous opportunities to learn or practice them.

2. The history of Central Park East is described in, *The Power of Their Ideas*, by Deborah Meier (1995).

3. In some countries, students stay with the same teacher and the class for the first four years of their primary school education. This organizational structure which offers considerable communal continuity seems especially beneficial for young students.

4. There are many local efforts at school reform that have been successful, such as James Comer's, School Development Program, Henry Levin's Accelerated Schools, and Theodore Sizer's Coalition of Essential Schools. Our interest is not to review each effort or major legislation such as Chicago School Reform, but rather to cite specific examples of school reform that seem particularly consistent with the output-driven model. As we stated earlier, public school choice is essential in the output-driven model, therefore, we have focused primarily on school organizational reforms that include public school choice.

References

Apple, M.W. 1993. *Official Knowledge: Democratic Education in a Conservative Age.* New York: Routledge.

Barr, Rebecca and Robert Dreeben. 1983. *How Schools Work.* Chicago: University of Chicago Press.

Becker, Betsy Jane. 1990. "Coaching for the Scholastic Aptitude Test: Further Synthesis and Appraisal." *Review of Educational Research* 60(3): 373-417.

Berliner, David and Bruce Biddle. 1995. *The Manufactured Crisis: Myths, Fraud, and the Attack on America'a Public Schools.* Redding, MA: Addison-Wesley Publishing Company.

Bierlein, Louann and Lori Mulholland. 1995. "Understanding Charter Schools." Position Paper, Bloomington: Phi Delta Kappa Educational Foundation.

Bidwell, Charles E. 1965. "The School as a Formal Organization." In J. G. March (Ed.), *Handbook of Organizations* (pp. 972-1022). Chicago: Rand McNally & Co.

Bishop, John. 1991. "A Strategy for Achieving Excellence in Secondary Education: The Role of State Government." Paper presented at the Chief State School Offices Summer Institute.

Brodt, Bonita. l996. "Some Say Kids Don't Take Tests Seriously." *Chicago Tribune.* November 11 (p.1).

Bronfenbrenner, U., Peter McClelland, E. Wethington, P. Moen and S.J. Ceci. 1996. *The State of Americans: This Generation and the Next.* The Free Press: New York.

Boyer, Ernest L. 1987. *College: The Undergraduate Experience in America.* New York: Harper and Row, Publishers.

Brody, Linda E., and Camilla Persson Benbow. 1990. "Effects of High School Coursework and Time on SAT Scores." *Journal of Educational Psychology* 82(4): 866-875.

Bryk, Anthony S., and Mary E. Driscoll. 1988. *The School as Community: Theoretical Foundations, Contextual Influences, and Consequences for Students and Teachers.* Chicago: The University of Chicago Benton Center for Curriculum and Instruction.

Bryk, Anthony S., Valerie E. Lee, and Peter B. Holland. 1993. *Catholic Schools and the Common Good.* Cambridge: Harvard University Press.

Bryk, Anthony S., and Stephen W. Raudenbush. 1992. *Hierarchical Linear Models: Applications And Data Analysis Methods.* Newbury Park, CA: Sage Publications.

Bryk, Anthony S., and Sharon G. Rollow. 1992. "The Chicago Experiment: Enhanced Democratic Participation as a Lever for School Improvement." *Issues in Restructuring Schools, Fall, l992.* Madison, WI: Center on Organization and Restructuring Schools.

Chandler, A. D. 1962. *Strategies and Structure: Chapters in the History of the Industrial Enterprise.* Cambridge, MA: Harvard University Press.

Clark, Jon (Ed.). 1996. *James S. Coleman.* London: Falmer.

Cohen, David. 1995. "What is the System in Systemic Reform?" *Educational Researcher* 24 (9): 11-17.

Cohen, D.K., M. McLaughlin, and J.E. Talbert (Eds.). 1993. *Teaching for Understanding: Challenges for Policy and Practice.* San Francisco: Jossey-Bass.

Cohen, Michael. 1983. "Instructional, Management and Social Conditions in Effective Schools." In A. O. Webb and L. D. Webb (Eds.), *School Finance And School Improvement: Linkages In The 1980's.* Cambridge: Ballinger.

Coleman, James S. 1961. *The Adolescent Society: The Social Life of the Teenager and Its Impact on Education.* New York: The Free Press.

Coleman, James S. 1988. "Social Capital in the Creation of Human Capital." *American Journal of Sociology* 94: 95-120.

Coleman, James S. 1990. *Foundations of Social Theory.* Cambridge: The Belknap Press of Harvard University Press.

Coleman, James S., Ernest Q. Campbell, Carol J. Hobson, James McPartland, Alexander M. Mood, Frederick D. Weinfeld, and Robert L. York. 1966. *Equality of Educational Opportunity.* Washington, D.C.: U.S. Government Printing Office.

Coleman, James S., and Thomas Hoffer. 1987. *Public and Private High Schools: The Impact of Communities.* New York: Basic Books.

Cooper, Thomas C. 1987. "Foreign Language Study and SAT-Verbal Scores." *The Modern Language Journal* 71: 381-387.

CORS. 1991. "Hidden Supports in School Restructuring." *Issues in Restructuring Schools*, Fall 1991. Madison, WI: Center on Organization and Restructuring of Schools.

Crouse, James. 1985. "Does the SAT Help Colleges Make Better Selection Decisions?" *Harvard Educational Review* 55: 195-219.

Crouse, James, and Dale Trusheim. 1991. "How Colleges Can Correctly Determine Selection Benefits from the SAT." *Harvard Educational Review* 61: 125-147.

Crouse, James, and Dale Trusheim. 1988. *The Case Against the SAT.* Chicago: University of Chicago Press.

Darling-Hammond, Linda. 1994. "National Standards and Assessments: Will They Improve Education?" *American Journal of Education* 102 (4).

Darling-Hammond, Linda. 1995. "Restructuring Schools for Students Success." *Deadalus* 124 (2): 153-162.

Dewey, John. 1943 (1956). *The School and Society.* Chicago: The University of Chicago Press.

Eckstein, Max A., and Harold J. Noah. 1993. *Secondary School Examinations: International Perspectives on Policies and Practice.* New Haven, Conn.: Yale University Press.

Elley, W.B. 1992. *How in the World Do Students Read?* Hamburg, Germany: The International Association for the Evaluation of Educational Achievement.

Firestone, W. A. 1994. "Redesigning Teacher Salary Systems for Educational Reform." *American Educational Research Journal* 31 (3): 549-574.

Frankel, M.R., L. Kohnke, D. Buonanno, and R. Touranggeau. 1981. *HS&B Base Year Sample Design Report.* Chicago: NORC.

Fuhrman, S. H. 1993. "Politics of Coherence." In S. H. Fuhrman (Ed.), *Designing Coherent Education Policy* (pp.1-34). California: Jossey-Bass.

Fulton, John D. 1995. *1995 Annual AMS-IMS-MAA Survey (First Report): Report of the 1995 Survey of New Doctoral Recipients.*

Gibbins, Neil, and Robert Bickel. 1991. "Comparing Public and Private High Schools Using Three SAT Data Sets." *The Urban Review* 23: 101-115.

Glass, G. and D. Hopkins. 1984. *Statistical Methods in Education and Psychology.* Englewood Cliffs, NJ: Prentis Hall.

Good, Thomas L., and Jere E. Brophy. 1986. "School Effects." In Merlin C. Wittrock (Ed.), *Handbook of Research on Teaching*, Third Edition (pp. 570-602). New York: Macmillan.

Gordon, Charles W. 1957. *The Social System of the High School.* Glencoe, IL: The Free Press.

Grant, Gerald. 1988. *The World We Created at Hamilton High.* Cambridge: Harvard University Press.

Hallinan, Maureen T. (Ed.). 1995. *Restructuring Schools: Promising Practices and Policies.* New York: Plenum Press.

Hallinger, Phillip, and Joseph F. Murphy. 1986. "The Social Context of Effective Schools." *American Journal of Education* 94 (3): 328-355.

Hanford, George H. 1985. "Yes, the SAT Does Help Colleges." *Harvard Educational Review* 55: 324-331.

Hauser, Robert M. 1993. "The Decline in College Entry among African Americans: Findings in Search of Explanations." In Sniderman, Tetlock, and Carmines (Eds.), *Prejudice, Politics, and the American Dilemma*. Stanford, CA: Stanford University Press.

Hewlett, Sylvia A. 1991. *When the Bough Breaks: The Cost of Neglecting Our Children.* New York: Basic Books.

House of Representatives, United States Congress. 1994. *Goals 2000: Educate America Act.* 103rd Congress, Washington, D.C.

Husen, Torsten (Ed.). 1967. *International Study of Achievement in Mathematics*, Vol. 2. Stockholm: Almqvist and Wicksell.

Ingels, Steven, Leslie Scott, J.T. Lindmark, Martin Frankel, and S.L. Myers. 1992. *Nels: 88 First Follow-Up Data File User's Manuals, 1992.*

Ingels, Steven, Leslie Scott, and Martin Frankel. 1996. *National Education Longitudinal Study of 1988-94 Sampling Design, Weighting and Estimation Report.* Washington, D.C.: U.S. Department of Education Office of Educational Research and Improvement.

Jackson, Rex. 1980. "The Scholastic Aptitude Test: A Response to Slack and Porter's 'Critical Appraisal.'" *Harvard Educational Review* 50 (3): 382-387.

Jencks, Christopher, and James Crouse. 1982. "Should We Relabel the SAT ... Or Replace It?" *Phi Delta Kappan* 63: 659-663.

Johnson, S.M. 1990. *Teachers at Work: Achieving Success in Our Schools.* New York: Basic Books.

Kariya, Takehiko, and James E. Rosenbaum. 1987. "Self-Selection in Japanese Junior High Schools: A Longitudinal Study of Students' Educational Plans." *Sociology of Education* 60: 168-180.

Keller, Dana, James Crouse, and Dale Trushiem. 1994. "The Effects of College Grade Adjustments on the Predictive Validity and Utility of SAT Scores." *Research in Higher Education* 35(2): 195-208.

Kohlberg, Lawrence. 1980. "High School Democracy and Educating for a Just Society." In Ralph L. Mosher (Ed.), *Moral Education: A First Generation of Research and Development* (pp. 20-49). New York: Praeger.

LaPointe, A.E., N.A. Mead, and J.M. Askew. 1992a. *Learning Mathematics, The International Assessment of Educational Progress*, Report no. 22-CAEP-01. Princeton, N.J.: Educational Testing Service.

LaPointe, A.E., N.A. Mead, and J.M.Askew. 1992b. *Learning Science*. Princeton, NJ: Educational Testing Service, The International Assessment of Educational Progress, Report No. 22-CAEP-02.

LaPointe, V., W. Jordan, J.M. McPartland, and D.P Towns. 1996. "The Talent Development High School: Essential Components." Baltimore, MD and Washington, D.C.: Center for Research on the Education of Students Placed at Risk.

Lee, Valerie and Julia Smith. 1995. "Effects of High School Restructuring and Size on Gains in Achievement Engagement for Early Secondary School Students." *Sociology of Education* 68 (4).

Lightfoot, Sara L. 1983. *The Good High School*. New York: Basic Books.

Linn, Robert. 1993. "Educational Assessment: Expanded Expectations and Challenges." *Educational Evaluation and Policy Analysis* 15 (1): 1-16.

Linn, Robert, and Eva L. Baker. 1995. "What Do International Assessments Imply for World-Class Standards? *Educational Evaluation and Policy Analysis* 17 (4): 405-418.

Lortie, D. 1975. *Schoolteachers: A Sociological Study*. Chicago: University of Chicago Press.

McDill, Edward L., Gary Natriello, and Aaron M. Pallas. 1986. "A Population at Risk: Potential Consequences of Tougher School Standards for Student Dropouts." *American Journal of Education* 94: 135-181.

McLaughlin, M.W. and L. Shepard. 1995. *Improving Education through Standards-Based Education Reform*. Stanford, California: The National Academy of Education.

Mackie, Gerry. 1991. *The Rise and Fall of the Forest Workers' Cooperative of the Pacific Northwest*. Unpublished Master's Theses. University of Oregon.

Manno, Bruno V. 1994. "Outcome-Based Education: Miracle Cure or Plague?" Indianapolis: Hudson Briefing Paper No. 165.

Medrich, Elliott and Jeanne Griffith. 1992. "International Mathematics and Science Assessment: What Have We Learned?" Research and Development Report. Berkeley, CA: MPR Associates.

Meier, Deborah. 1995. *The Power of Their Ideas*. Boston: Beacon Press.

Mirel, Jeffrey, and David Angus. 1994. "High Standards for All." *American Educator* 18(2): 4-42.

Murphy, Joseph F., Marsha Weil, Philip Hallinger, and Alexis Mitman. 1982. "Academic Press: Translating High Expectations into School Policies and Classroom Practices." *Educational Leadership* 40: 22-26.

Murray, Charles, and R.J. Herrnstein. 1992. "The Education Impasse." *The Public Interest* no. 166: 32-56.

NASSP. 1992. A Leader's Guide to School Restructuring: A Special Report of the NASSP Comission on Restructuring. Reston, VA: National Association of Secondary School Principals.

National Center for Education Statistics. 1987. *High School and Beyond: 1980 Sophomore Cohort 88, Third Follow-up, Data File User's Manual.* Washington, D.C.: NCES.

National Center for Education Statistics. 1992. *National Educational Longitudinal Study of 1988: First Follow-up Student File, Users' Manual.* Washington, D.C.: NCES.

National Center for Education Statistics. 1994. *National Educational Longitudinal Study of 1988: Second Follow-up Student File, Users' Manual.* Washington, D.C.: NCES.

National Center for Education Statistics. 1995. *Who Can Play? An Examination of NCAA's Proposition 16.* Washington, D.C.: NCES.

National Comission on Excellence in Education. 1983. *A Nation at Risk.* Washington, D.C.: U.S. Department of Education.

National Council of Teachers of Mathematics. 1991. *Professional Standards for Teaching Mathematics.* Reston, VA: National Council of Teachers of Mathematics.

National Council of Teachers of Mathematics. 1995. *Assessment Standards for School Mathematics.* Reston, VA: National Council of Teachers of Mathematics.

National Council on Education Standards and Testing. 1992. *Raising Standards for American Education: A Report to Congress, the Secretary of Education, the National Education Goals Panel, and the American People.* Washington, D.C.

National Education Goals Panel. 1991. *The National Education Goals Report.* Washington, D.C.: Author.

National Science Foundation. 1994. *Women, Minorities, and Persons with Disabilities in Science and Engineering: 1994.* NSF 94-333.

NCEA Research and Development Report. 1992. *International Mathematics and Science Assessments: What Have We Learned?* Washington, D.C.

Neill, A. S. 1960. *Summerhill: A Radical Approach to Child Rearing.* New York: Hart Publishing Company, Inc.

Oakes, Jeannie. 1985. *Keeping Track: How Schools Structure Inequality.* New Haven: Yale University Press.

Pace, R. Wayne, and George G. Stern. 1958. "An Approach to the Measurement of Psychological Characteristics of College Environments." *Journal of Educational Psychology* 49: 269-277.

Pallas, Aaron M., and Karl L. Alexander. 1983. "Sex Differences in Quantitative SAT Performance: New Evidence on the Differential Coursework Hypothesis." *American Educational Research Journal* 20(2): 165-182.

Powell, Arthur G., Eleanor Farrar, and David K. Cohen. 1985. *The Shopping Mall High School: Winners And Losers In The Educational Marketplace.* Boston: Houghton Mifflin Co.

Powell, Brian and Lala C. Steelman. 1984. "Variations in State SAT Performance: Meaningful or Misleading." *Harvard Educational Review* 54 (4): 389-412.

Power, F. Clark, Ann Higgens, and Lawrence Kohlberg. 1989. *Lawrence Kohlberg's Approach to Moral Education*. New York: Columbia University Press.

Ravitch, Diane. 1993. "Launching a Revolution in Standards and Assessments." *Phi Delta Kappan* 74 (10): 767-772.

Ravitch, Diane. 1995. *National Standards in American Education: A Citizen's Guide*. Washington, D.C.: Brookings.

Rasinski, Kenneth A., Steven J. Ingels, Donald A. Rock, Judith M. Pollack, and Shi-Chang Wu. 1993. *America's High School Sophomores: A Ten Year Comparison, 1980-1990*. Washington, D.C.: U.S. Department of Education. NCES 92-087.

Rock, D.P., J.M. Pollack and P. Quinn. 1995. *Psychometric Report for the NELS: 88 Base Year Through Second Follow-Up*. Washington, D.C.: U.S. Department of Education.

Rodriguez, Richard. 1982. *Hunger of Memory: The Education of Richard Rodriguez*. New York: Bantam Books.

Rutter, Michael, B. Maughan, Peter Mortimore, John Ouston, and A. Smith. 1979. *Fifteen Thousand Hours: Secondary Schools and Their Effects on Children*. Cambridge: Harvard University Press.

Schiller, Kathryn S. 1994. "When Do Catholic Schools Matter? New Evidence from NELS:88." Presented at the American Sociological Association meetings in Los Angeles.

Sedlak, Michael W., Christopher W. Wheeler, Diana C. Pullin, and Philip A. Cusick. 1986. *Selling Students Short: Classroom Bargains and Academic Reform in the American High School*. New York: Teachers College Press.

Sergiovanni, Thomas. 1994. *Building Community in Schools*. San Francisco: Jossey-Bass.

Shouse, Roger C. 1994. *Academic Orientation and School Society: The Meaning and Importance of Academic Press*. Unpublished doctoral dissertation. The University of Chicago.

Sizer, Theodore R. 1984. *Horace's Compromise: The Dilemma of the American High School*. Boston: Houghton Mifflin.

Slack, Warner V., and Douglas Porter. 1980. "The Scholastic Aptitude Test: A Critical Appraisal." *Harvard Educational Review* 50(2): 154-174.

Smith, Marshall, and Jennifer O'Day. 1991. "Systemic School Reform." In S. H. Fuhrman and Betty Malen (Eds.). *The Politics of Curriculum and Testing* (pp.233-267). London: Falmer Press, Politics of Education Association, 1990 Yearbook.

Snyder, Thomas D., and Charlene M. Hoffman. 1995. *Digest of Education Statistics 1995*. NCES 95-029. Washington, D.C.: U.S. Department of Education, Office of Educational Research and Improvement.

Steinberg, L, B.B. Brown and S.M. Dornbusch. 1996. *Beyond The Classroom*. New York: Simon and Schuster.

Stevenson, David Lee, and David P. Baker. 1992. "Shadow Education Allocation in Formal Schooling: Transition to University in Japan." *American Journal of Sociology* 97: 1639-57.

Stevenson, David Lee, Kathryn S. Schiller, and Barbara Schneider. 1994. "Sequences of Opportunities for Learning." *Sociology of Education* 67: 184-198.

Stevenson, David Lee, and David P. Baker. l991 "State Control of the Curriculum and Classroom Instruction." *Sociology of Education* 64: 1-10.

Stevenson, David Lee. 1995. "Goals 2000 and Local Reform." *Teachers College Record* 96 (3).

Stevenson, Harold W., James W. Stigler, Shin-ying Lee, G. William Lucker, Seiro Kitamura, and Chen-chin Hsu. 1985. "Cognitive Performance and Academic Achievement of Japanese, Chinese, and American Children." *Child Development* 56: 718-734.

Stevenson, Harold W., Shin-ying Lee, and James W. Stigler. 1986. "Mathematics Achievement of Chinese, Japanese, and American Children." *Science* 231: 693-699.

Stevenson, Harold W., Chuansheng Chen, and Shin-ying Lee. 1993. "Mathematics Achievement of Chinese, Japanese, and American Children: Ten Years Later." *Science* 259: 53-58.

Swanson, Christopher and Barbara Schneider. 1996. "Students on the Move: Residential and Educational Mobility in America's Schools." Manuscript in Preparation. University of Chicago.

Taylor, Catherine S., and Susan B. Nolen. 1996. "What Does The Psychometrician's Classroom Look Like?: Reframing Assessment Concepts in the Context of Learning." In Gene V. Glass (Ed.), *Education Policy Analysis Archives* 4 (17): ISSN 1068-2341.

Wainer, Howard, and Linda S. Steinberg. 1992. "Sex Differences in Performance on the Mathematics Section of the Scholastic Aptitude Test: A Bidirectional Validity Study." Harvard Educational Review 62 (3): 323-336.

Waller, Willard. 1932 (1967). *The Sociology Of Teaching*. New York: John Wiley & Sons.

Weber, Max. 1947. *The Theory of Social and Economic Organization* (A.M. Henderson and Talcott Parsons, Trans.). New York: Oxford.

Whelage, Gary, R. Rutter, A. Smith, Nancy Lesko and Ricardo Fernandez. 1989. *Reducing The Risk: Schooling as Communities of Support*. Bristol, PA: Falmer.

Willis, Scott. Winter 1996. "Foreign Languages: Learning to Communicate in the Real World." *Curriculum Update*, 1-4, 6-8.

Wong, K. 1995. "Can the Big-City School System be Governed?" in P. Cookson and B. Schneider (Eds.), *Transforming Schools*. New York: Garland.

Worthington, Rogers. 1996. "Facing Their Biggest Test." *Chicago Tribune*, December 1 (p.C4).

About the Authors

James S. Coleman was a world-renowned professor of sociology at The University of Chicago. His scholarly career was devoted to the creation and use of new social science methodology and theory to illuminate major issues in public policy. His main contributions lay in sociological theory--including the analysis of social change, collective action, and rational choice--the sociology of education, and public policy. Dr. Coleman's early research on schools and schooling helped shape government policy on racial integration and school busing. The best known product of the research was "Equality of Educational Opportunity," commonly known as the Coleman Report (1966). Dr. Coleman's later studies compared the relative efficacy of public and private elementary schools. He co-authored *High School Achievement: Public, Catholic and Private Schools Compared* (1982, with Thomas Hoffer and Sally Kilgore) and *Public and Private High Schools: The Impact of Communities* (1987, with Hoffer). He spent much of the last two decades of his life working on sociological theory. These efforts culminated in his 1990 book, *Foundations of Social Theory*. The book, which is already considered a classic, applies a rational choice approach to social behavior, showing how individual choices are affected by social norms, peer pressure, a desire to emulate leaders, and other group influences.

Barbara Schneider is a senior social scientist at the National Opinion Research Center and The University of Chicago. She has published numerous articles, chapters, monographs, and two books on educational policy, parental involvement, and school choice. *Parents, Their Children, and Schools* (1993, co-edited with James S. Coleman) examines the resources available to parents and the actions parents can take to further their children's education. This book was the first intensive, comprehensive study of parent actions based on major survey data from the National Education Longitudinal Study of 1988--a national survey of 26,000 8th graders and their parents, teachers, and school administrators. Her second book, *Transforming Schools* (1995, co-edited with Peter W. Cookson Jr.), is a collection of essays written by leading educational sociologists who examine some of the major problems in American education today and review several different solutions. Dr. Schneider's current research is learning how adolescents formulate ideas about work and postsecondary education plans. This work, funded by the Alfred P. Sloan Foundation, is a five-year longitudinal study of junior high and high school students. She is currently co-authoring with David Stevenson a new book, *Finding One's Way* which compares the lives of adolescents in the 1950s and the 1990s.

Stephen Plank is an associate research scientist at the Center for Social Organization of Schools and an adjunct professor of sociology, both at Johns Hopkins University. He is the author of several articles and book chapters on topics including school choice and students' career interest formation. His current research includes an examination of the transition from high school to postsecondary education and/or work, with a focus on students' access to information networks and guidance services. He is also involved in several studies of adolescents' formation of career interests. His research interests involve network analysis, small group processes, and the stratifying mechanisms of schooling.

Kathryn S. Schiller is a visiting assistant professor in the Department of Sociology at the University of Notre Dame. Her specialties are sociology of education and research methodology. She is the author of several articles and book chapters relating to sequences of opportunities for learning and school choice as a form of parental involvement. Her research interests focus on the constraints and opportunities created for individuals by organizational structures and practices. In addition to the design of incentive systems, her current work explores how variations in organizational links between middle schools and high schools affect students' access to educational opportunities. One of her other collaborative projects focuses on ways in which state policies can produce changes in school practices over time.

Roger Shouse is an assistant professor of education policy studies at the Pennsylvania State University, College of Education. A middle school and high school teacher for over 10 years in both suburban and inner city schools, his current research focuses on the complex effects of school socioeconomic status, organizational culture, and curricular and instructional practices on student achievement.

Huayin Wang is a sociology Ph.D. student at The University of Chicago. His research interests include adolescent culture, significant others, preference formations, and rational choice theories.

Index